"FAITHFUL, FIRM, AND TRUE"

"Faithful, Firm, and True"

African American Education in the South

Titus Brown

Mercer
University
Press
MMII

ISBN 0-86554-752-1 (cloth)
MUP/H562
ISBN 0-86554-777-7 (paper)
MUP/P219

© 2002 Mercer University Press
1400 Coleman Avenue
Macon, Georgia 31207
All rights reserved

First Edition.
2nd Printing, February 2006.

The paper used in this publication meets the minimum
requirements of American National Standard for
Information Sciences—Permanence of Paper for Printed
Library Materials, ANSI Z39.48-1992.

Library of Congress Cataloging-in-Publication Data

Brown, Titus.
 Faithful, firm, and true : African American education in the South /
Titus Brown.— 1st ed.
   p. cm.
Includes bibliographical references (p.   ) and index.
 ISBN 0-86554-752-1 (hardcover : alk. paper)—ISBN 0-86554-777-7
(pbk. : alk. paper)
 1. African Americans—Education (Secondary)—Georgia—History.
 2. African American educators—Southern States—History. I. Title.
 LC2779 .B76 2002
 373.182996'073—dc21

                                                              2002004817

CONTENTS

LIST OF TABLES

PREFACE

From Reconstruction until well into the twentieth century, the American Missionary Association was the most significant agency engaged in training African Americans in Central Georgia, and especially in Macon. The association, based in New York, provided the best education available to black youths in Macon, with an integrated faculty that taught equality by example. Its school trained the teachers needed to teach thousands of black students from the Jim Crow era through the beginnings of the Civil Rights movement.

During its development from unheated schoolrooms to the premier secondary institution for African Americans in Central Georgia, Ballard Normal School, a joint effort of the black community and the AMA, overcame poverty, disease, white hostility, and a paucity of qualified teachers and funds. From its inception at the end of the Civil War, the school produced students who fulfilled the promise of freedom and education. Early graduates Lucy Craft Laney and William Scarborough were among Atlanta University's first graduating class in the 1870s, and Ballard's continuing excellence later produced renowned novelist John Oliver Killens, class of 1933.

The AMA's educational program at Macon emphasized "religion, patriotism, morality, and an industrious black citizenry." To increase the number of black teachers, in 1868 the AMA instituted a normal curriculum at its newly opened Lewis High, which soon became a model teacher training school.

When the state of Georgia began to assume responsibility for public education, the AMA briefly permitted the Macon School Board in 1872 to designate Lewis High a public school for blacks. A basic difference in philosophy between the AMA and the school board over segregation and the standard of education being offered led the AMA to resume control in 1875. In 1888 the AMA built a new, larger facility, renamed Ballard Normal School. Ballard fostered an academic course of study for its students. While Ballard taught the use of hand tools, the school did not follow the Hampton or Tuskegee models or the educational principles espoused by Booker T. Washington and Samuel Armstrong, which advanced an almost exclusively industrial curriculum.

With no mandated state support for secondary education until 1912, the Ballard school played an important role in educating African Americans in Central Georgia well into the twentieth century. Further, while Georgia and other Southern states began to expand educational opportunities for white children in the 1920s, they failed to provide the same arrangements for African-American youth. Except for a few overcrowded, dilapidated buildings for training African-American teachers, funding for black education in the South was left largely to philanthropic organizations and private efforts. The only avenues for a high school education open to Georgia blacks were the state's seventeen four-year private schools, which enrolled approximately 2,000 students. Besides being a purveyor of knowledge and values, the Ballard school served as a hub for visiting dignitaries and as an activity center for Macon's segregated black community.

Until the 1940s, Ballard was one of the few accredited secondary schools for blacks in Georgia. Led by principals such as George Burrage and Raymond von Tobel, the students thrived, and the school not only survived but excelled. Public schools for black students in Bibb County ended at grade six, and fully accredited Ballard offered the only opportunity for a high school education. Many of the students who completed Ballard's four-year college-preparatory course pursued higher education. Those completing the normal program became teachers.

What follows is a narrative history of how black initiative, Southern race relations, and a "Yankee" value system of religion, morality, and paternalism came together in a schoolroom in Macon, Georgia, beginning in 1865. Ballard Normal School reflects the determination of the AMA to assist the African-American community of Macon in providing high quality education for its youth. Throughout its long history, its students combined high moral character, superior scholarship, and careful, honest, and efficient work in the spirit of their school anthem, "Faithful, Firm, and True." To this day, Macon boasts many Ballardites who went on to make significant contributions to their professions, their communities, and society at large.

I wish to express my deepest appreciation and thanks to several history faculty members at Florida State University, particularly Professor Joe M. Richardson, whose guidance was inspiring as well as instructional, and to Professors Neil B. Betten, Charles E. Billings, Maxine D. Jones, William R. Jones, and William W. Rogers for their valuable comments on the text.

I wish to express my gratitude to the National Endowment for the Humanities and to Israel Tribble, Jr., president of the Florida Educational Fund (formerly McKnight Fund), for faculty development awards that enabled me to pursue my research.

I am indebted to the library staffs of Florida A&M and Florida State universities as well as the Amistad Research Center, Tulane University, and the Washington Memorial Library in Macon, Georgia. At Florida A&M University I also wish to thank Professor James N. Eaton, Black Archives, and my colleagues in the Department of History and Political Science for their support during this project. Many thanks, too, to Andrew M. Manis at Mercer University Press for his invaluable comments on the manuscript.

Many thanks to my family and friends for their continuing encouragement and support. Finally, I wish to express a special thanks to Margaret Barlow for her assistance in completing this project.

Ballard Normal School, founded in 1865. The American
Missionary Association financed the construction in 1914 of a
new building for Macon's Ballard School (pictured above). It
stood on a new campus on Forest Avenue, two miles from the
school's original site.

This senior class photograph, from the early 1920s, includes
both students and faculty.

Athletics were a major part of student extracurricular life at
Ballard Normal School. The winning records of several of its
high school teams over the years enhanced the school's
reputation both locally and statewide. Above, the baseball
team of 1909, and below, team captains of the 1924-25 teams.

Connecticut native Raymond G. von Tobel spent most of his career as principal of the Ballard Normal School for African-American students in Macon, Georgia. His effective leadership there led one AMA official to describe him as the "New England missionary at best."

A young William Scarborough who attended Lincoln Free Schools in 1865-1868 and two years at Lewis High before enrolling as one of the first student and graduate of Atlanta University and then Oberlin College in Ohio. He later taught Greek and Latin at Wilberforce University in Ohio, prior to becoming president of that institution.

The Ballard School band.

Northern whites who taught at Ballard Normal including Mrs. Mounts, von Tobel, and Tuttle.

Elementary school students at Ballard.

Ballard Normal play, circa 1949.

Manual training at Ballard, although Ballard taught industrial
education for its practical value it never replaced Ballard's
Liberal Arts tradition.

Ballard Normal had a biracial faculty throughout its existence
until it became public in 1942. Above, the faculty for
1925-1926.

Ballard Students, 1913.

Ballard Glee Club—1910;
Gertrude Jackson (middle row on
right).

Class of 1930 from left to right: Moneta Dallas Price, Kathleen Cook Pitts, and Louise Dallas Leonard.

Ballard female students.

CHAPTER 1[1]

ORIGINS OF AFRICAN-AMERICAN EDUCATION IN MACON, GEORGIA 1865–1866

Historians have observed that before the Civil War drew to a close, Northern philanthropic organizations had begun to establish freedmen schools and to supply teachers from the North and Midwest, mostly women, who brought with them a "Yankee" value system of religion, patriotism, and morality. The organizations that remained cooperated with Republican politicians; the Bureau of Refugees, Freedmen, and Abandoned Lands (called the Freedmen's Bureau); and the African-American community. Despite the attention of historians to the role played by Northern aid societies in supplying teachers and equipment and the Freedmen's bureau's role in procuring buildings, few studies have acknowledged the initiative blacks took to build and sustain their own educational institutions. This chapter attempts to fill this gap in the literature. Its focal point is the role of Afro-Maconites who, in their first year of freedom, provided the atmosphere for the American Missionary Association (AMA) to impose its Northern-slanted religious and educational value system.[2]

---

[1] This chapter appeared in a slightly altered form in *The Journal of South west Georgia History* 11 (Fall 1996).

[2] Jacqueline Jones, *Soldiers of Light and Love: Northern Teachers and Georgia Blacks, 1865–1873* (Chapel Hill: University of North Carolina Press, 1980) 5,

Almost as soon as they were emancipated, freedmen in the South began to establish schools wherever buildings and teachers could be secured. The first teachers were ex-slaves who were ministers, grocers, and artisans. As Joseph Reidy wrote, "Given the magnitude of the task before them and the modesty of the resources at their disposal, freedpeople necessarily turned to outside financial assistance." Much of this assistance came from the North. In the summer of 1865, the Western Freedmen's Aid Commission, in cooperation with the Freedmen's Bureau, went to Macon, Georgia, to establish schools for freedmen. The Western Freedmen's Aid Commission was formed to assist in the education of freedmen after a schism occurred within the Contraband Relief Commission of Cincinnati on 19 January 1863.[3]

69–70; Ronald E. Butchart, *Northern Schools, Southern Blacks, and Reconstruction: Freedmen's Bureau Education 1862–1875* (Westport CT: Greenwood Press, 1980) 11–12; James D. Anderson, *The Education of Blacks in the South, 1865–1935* (Chapel Hill: University of North Carolina Press, 1988) 11–12. Joe M. Richardson, *Christian Reconstruction: The American Missionary Association and Southern Blacks, 1861–1890* (Athens: University of Georgia Press, 1986) 190, 202; Paul Cimbala, "Making Good Yankees: The Freedmen's Bureau and Education in Reconstruction Georgia, 1865–1870," *Atlanta Historical Journal* 29 (Fall 1985): 5.

[3] Augustus Field Beard, *A Crusade of Brotherhood: A History of the American Missionary Association* (Boston: Pilgrim Press, 1909) 141, 160; Fred L. Brownlee, *New Day Ascending* (Boston: Pilgrim Press, 1946) 138–40. The Freedmen's Bureau, which operated from 12 March 1865 through 31 August 1871, expended approximately $306,000 for freedmen education in Georgia. George R. Bentley, *A History of the Freedmen's Bureau* (Philadelphia: University of Pennsylvania, 1955) 171; Richard R. Wright, *A Brief Historical Sketch of Negro Education in Georgia* (Savannah: Robinson Printing House, 1894) 26–27; Henry L. Swint, *The Northern Teacher in the South, 1862–1870* (Nashville: Vanderbilt University Press, 1941) 20. Discussed in William Cole and Lavinia Martin to George L. Eberhart, 19 October 1865, Teacher Monthly School Reports, Bureau of Refugees, Freedmen and Abandoned Lands, Educational Division, Georgia; hereafter cited as BRFAL-Ed. Ga.; and Susan F. Presley, "A Past to Cherish—A Future to Fulfill, Lewis High—Ballard Normal School, 1865–1900" (Master's thesis, Georgia Southern University, 1992) 62–63; Joseph P. Reidy, *From Slavery*

Professor John Ogden of the Tennessee branch of the Western Freedmen's Aid Commission arrived in Macon on 12 July 1865 to begin arrangements for opening four freedmen schools in the city. Two days later, the *Macon Daily Telegraph* printed his statement:

> These schools have been duly organized in this City under the auspices of the Western Freedmen's Aid Commission by the employment of two permanent and ten assistant or temporary teachers—the latter to remain until permanent teachers can be secured.
>
> It is the design of the superintending agent to make these schools worthy of the confidence of the public. To this end he will call about him the best teachers that can be had.
>
> It is not the design in the organization of these schools to make them a medium through which to appeal to the bad passions or prejudices of the freed people, or to incite animosity and ill feeling towards their former masters, neither to excite or encourage undue expectations in regard to the new relations in which the black man now finds himself placed, but rather to allay ill feeling, to encourage and enforce, as far as possible, habits of industry and honesty, kindness and forbearance—to give the young, in particular, the advantages of an education, as a matter of government policy, as well as of high principle, in a word to make men and women of those who have hitherto been regarded as property.
>
> In this we are sustained by the government of the United States; and under its sanction, and the approbation of all good citizens, we hope and expect to succeed.

---

to Agrarian Capitalism in the Cotton Plantation South: Central Georgia, 1800–1880 (Chapel Hill: University of North Carolina Press, 1992) 171–73.

John Ogden
Agent, Western Freedmen's Aid Commission
Macon, Ga., July 12, 1865[4]

These early schools in Macon, held in four buildings owned by the black Baptist, Methodist, and Presbyterian churches, were staffed by local teachers, ten black and two white. After two months had elapsed, the Western Freedmen's Aid Commission sent Daniel Hough to evaluate the schools. Hough appraised the efforts of the freedmen teachers: "as well as I could expect teachers to do who have never been taught more than they have or who have no head [principal]." He also noted that many of the teachers, having received no compensation for their work, were at the starving point. In fact, Hough wrote to area headquarters in Tennessee, "Miss [Emeline] Kidd said as they had not heard from you from the time you went away, she thought you had deserted them, and began even to doubt of the existence of the Commission."[5]

After a careful review of the situation, Hough concluded that all looked well, "but we need a head, one good superintendent who could instruct the teachers." Hough held the position that all involved with freedmen education could benefit from "a man who understands superintending and drilling teachers."[6]

In the meantime, the teachers were suffering from lack of cash. "On account of extravagant rent," the teachers were constantly in need of food, clothing, and housing. Reverend W. H. Robert, Area Superintendent of Freedmen's Schools, reported to Gilbert L.

---

[4] *Macon Daily Telegraph*, 14 July 1865.

[5] The local black resident teachers were Lewis Smith, Henry Taylor, Lewis Williams, William Cole, John L. Bentley, Isaac L. Primus, Robert Mitchell, P. M. Sellars, Ella Watson, and Lavinia Martin. The two local white permanent teachers were Emeline Kidd and her mother, Mrs. Kidd. See Report of Freedmen's School for City of Macon, 25 October 1865, BRFAL-Ed. Ga. Daniel Hough to John Ogden, 29 September 1865, American Missionary Association Archives, Amistad Research Center, New Orleans, Louisiana; hereafter cited as AMAA.

[6] Hough to Ogden, 29 September 1965, AMAA.

Eberhart, superintendent of education under the Freedmen's Bureau, that the "salary of these teachers is small and they suffer because they cannot get it promptly; they need it now, everything is cash in advance that they buy and yet they have to wait and wait and suffer greatly for their just dues; can you help them out?"[7]

The Western Freedmen's Aid Commission had promised to pay the freedmen teachers in Macon twenty-five dollars per month, plus a special allowance of thirty cents per day for "rations." After working for four months, teacher William Cole wrote Superintendent Eberhart complaining that the teachers "have received but two months pay without the stipulated amount for rations." Parents of the students paid nothing, "as they [were] not able to pay to have their children taught." Moreover, inadequate funds prevented the school from obtaining uniform textbooks for students. Cole's class purchased its own books at a "very high price."[8]

The First Baptist Denomination Church provided the school building in which Cole taught at no cost to the bureau or the Freedmen's Aid Commission. In an effort to accommodate more students, Cole fitted a basement for a classroom at a cost of eighty-five dollars, which "Mr. Ogden promised to pay for on his return, but as he has not returned it has never been paid." One hundred twenty-four pupils of varied ages were enrolled. The students were instructed in the alphabet, spelling, reading, writing, and arithmetic. Cole's first class of fifteen girls ranged in age from twelve to eighteen. They used elementary spelling books and Willson's first and second readers.[9]

At Freedmen's School No. 4, African-American teachers John L. Bentley and Isaac L. Primus instructed 174 pupils. Bentley and Primus used a schoolhouse belonging to the Second African Baptist

---

[7] Ibid.; also Rev. W. H. Robert to G. L. Eberhart, 25 October 1865, Teacher Monthly School Reports, BRFAL-Ed. Ga.

[8] William Cole and Lavinia Martin to G. L. Eberhart, 19 October 1865, Teacher Monthly School Reports, BRFAL-Ed. Ga.

[9] Ibid.

Church of Macon. They were forced to ask parents for donations in order to improve school facilities, as "the house is in a very bad condition; it is very open and we have no stove or any other means of warming the school." Five pupils studied geography, while twenty-nine studied reading, twenty-seven arithmetic, and thirty-six the alphabet. Primus and Bentley based their lessons on the elementary spelling book of *McGuffey's Eclectic First Reader* and *Cornell's Grammar-School Geography*. The school session commenced at 8:00 a.m. with reading and prayer services; classes recessed from 11:30 a.m. to 12 noon and ended at 2:00 p.m.[10]

Another of the four Macon freedmen schools was taught by Lewis Smith, a local resident involved with the Georgia Educational Movement.[11] His classes included a total of 372 students, with almost equal numbers of males (184) and females (188). Unfortunately, little other information exists about Smith's school. Compared with reports from the other freedmen schools that opened in the immediate postwar years, Smith's report to Superintendent Eberhart is sketchy, altogether lacking in details.[12]

Within two months of their opening, overall enrollment in Macon's freedmen schools held firm at about 600 pupils. All schools were in "good order except number 1 and only a little noisy," Hough reported. "The progress for two months operation

---

[10] William Cole and Lavinia Martin, and John L. Bentley and Isaac Primus to G. L. Eberhart, 19 October 1865, Teacher Monthly School Reports, BRFAL-Ed. Ga. Like Freedmen's School No. 4, all of the freedmen's schools were numbered; however, other teachers at times did not indicate their school's number in their reports.

[11] Lewis Smith to G. L. Eberhart, 19 October 1865, Teacher Monthly School Reports, BRFAL-Ed. Ga. Information about this school also reported in *Loyal Georgian*, 20 January 1866, and *Proceedings of the Freedmen's Convention of Georgia*, 10 January 1866, Augusta, 4. In 1866 black Georgians met and organized the Georgia Educational Association and chose John E. Bryant as their president. Their goal was to create and sustain schools for blacks in each county and district in Georgia; their official organ was the *Loyal Georgian*, published in Augusta, with Bryant as editor.

[12] Ruth Currie-McDaniel, *Carpetbagger of Conscience: A Biography of John Emory Bryant* (Athens: University of Georgia Press, 1987) 57–65.

was remarkable as the children seem to be learning very fast." Instructional materials were in short supply, and the teachers used almost every kind of first reader, resulting in a lack of uniformity. Also, some were unable to accomplish much in writing technique for lack of writing slates.[13]

Even though many of the teachers were inadequately trained, there was great progress in the first few months after emancipation. Freedman teacher Robert Mitchell described his position well in a letter to Superintendent Eberhart. Mitchell wrote that although he did not consider himself a scholar or

> competent to teach school...yet I thought I could do some good to teach amongst the people of my color. I am a man that never was taught in school or any other place in all my life and yet I am called upon to do so important a work. On this I am not complaining but [simply] commenting on this glorious and all important work which has been committed to my charge.[14]

In fact, both Eberhart and Area Bureau Superintendent Rev. W. H. Robert had some doubts about the quality of instruction at Macon. Eberhart reported, "I learned that under the patronage of the Western Freedmen's Aid Association a few colored persons have opened schools in Macon, but they were of course equally as inefficient as those in Savannah." Reverend Robert noted that "these schools have been under the tuition of colored men and women except one (Mrs. Kidd) who have had no experience as teachers and hence it would have been useless to look for that proficiency in advancement which might have been expected under other and different circumstances." In view of these facts, Hough

---

[13] Daniel Hough to John Ogden, 29 September 1865, AMAA.
[14] Robert Mitchell to G. L. Eberhart, 25 October 1865, Teacher Monthly School Reports, BRFAL-Ed. Ga.

wrote to Eberhart, "I shall as soon as possible receive permission to make some changes in the teachers."[15]

The freedmen's desire to improve educational opportunities for their children was evident when W. B. Scott, an assistant to Eberhart, visited the various church schools in the city in late October. "At the solicitation of a large circle of the most intelligent colored people of this City," Scott wrote, "I drop you a few lines in regard to a first class school at this place." Scott was "confident" that such a school was needed in Macon and would be properly sustained. During his consultations with leading black citizens, he had detected both a need and a desire for "a first class teacher" who could teach a higher grade.[16]

In November 1865, four months after the freedmen schools had been opened, the Western Freedmen's Aid Commission transferred responsibility for the Macon schools to the American Missionary Association (AMA), an organization founded in 1839 by Congregational ministers and laymen as an antislavery organization. (By 1867 the organizations had merged.) In the years immediately following the Civil War, the AMA had concentrated on freedmen education. In fact, the organization dominated education for African Americans in Tennessee, Alabama, and Louisiana, and in Georgia it controlled schools for freedmen in all major cities except Columbus.[17]

Erastus Milo Cravath, acting on behalf of the association, arrived in Macon in December and established the Lincoln Home to house the teachers the AMA would be sending. At the same time, he secured permission from local black church officials to continue using their buildings for schools. E. P. Smith, AMA field secretary, described the preparations:

---

[15] G. L. Eberhart, Superintendent Report, 8 October 1866, BRFAL-Ed. Ga.; Rev. W. H. Robert to G. L. Eberhart, 25 October 1865, BRFAL-Ed. Ga.; Daniel Hough to John Ogden, 29 September 1865, AMAA.

[16] W. B. Scott to John Ogden, 20 October 1865, AMAA.

[17] Beard, *A Crusade of Brotherhood*, 31–32; Richardson, *Christian Reconstruction*, 37.

Mr. Cravath started from Nashville, last Thursday week, with a corps of ten teachers. He had previously secured a house for a "home" in Macon. On reaching the city, the company went directly to their quarters, and were most agreeably surprised to be welcomed to their home by a company of colored ladies who had learned of their coming, and had volunteered to make the house ready. Mr. Cravath says: "We found our home swept, secured, and garnished, and quite a number of the good people waiting and anxious to show their gratitude by any help they could render." It was an ovation delicately done, but done to purpose.

In the five churches (colored) of Macon, the ten teachers are to commence their work. Rev. Mr. Eddy will be missionary at large, and will undoubtedly extend the work in all directions from there, if we can get the means. The colored people are organized into a voluntary association, and will provide the rooms for schools, furnish fuel, and kindle the fires. Miss Martha D. Ayers, of Worcester, Mass., is to be the Matron of the Home. I trust you will get many voices of cheer from that apostolic band of twelve at Macon.[18]

The "Home" had been provided with the necessary articles that made for wholesome living, and all the newly imported teachers lived there. Maconite Emeline Kidd continued to live with her mother in the city. The cost to ready the teachers' "Home" reached a total of $388.55, which included purchase of a dining

---

[18] *20th Annual Report of the AMA*, 1866, 31. The early AMA arrangements in Macon are also discussed in Jones, *Soldiers of Light and Love*, 62; Erastus M. Cravath to Samuel Hunt, 15 December 1865, AMAA; *Macon Daily Telegraph*, 7 February 1866; and *American Missionary* 10 (March 1866): 62–63.

table, four washstands, fifteen chairs, blankets, bedsteads, muslin for sheets, wardrobes, and other needed articles.[19]

The AMA sent Rev. Hiram Eddy to superintend the Macon schools. One week after his arrival, he reported that "on the whole I am very favorably impressed in regard to the state of things in Macon." He was generally satisfied with the operation of the four church schools, although one was located in "an uncomfortable building without windows," where the only opening was the door, which had to be closed in cold weather.[20]

Cravath had reported earlier that the four churches had been put into good condition for the schools. Each school had two teachers, and classes averaged near forty pupils each, with more students expected. Cravath estimated an attendance of sixty per class within a few weeks. The new teachers adapted quickly, and Eddy wrote to AMA headquarters that "you could not have sent a better corps of teachers than you have here. They are intelligent, experienced and love their work." Eddy also was pleased to find that Cravath had "secured the hearty endorsement of some of the most prominent citizens, among whom is the mayor."[21]

Shortly after Eddy congratulated the AMA on its wise choice of workers, a crisis arose that pointed up the types of problems affecting many newly freed slaves. At the end of December 1865, a severe outbreak of smallpox occurred among African Americans, due in part to overcrowded housing and exposure to bad weather conditions. Many freedmen in Georgia had migrated from rural areas to larger towns, seeking employment as well as greater safety under the protection of federal officers. With little decent housing

---

[19] E. M. Cravath to Samuel Hunt, 15 December 1865, AMAA; "Bill of Articles Provided for Macon Home," 8 December 1865, AMAA.

[20] Hiram Eddy to Rev. M. E. Strieby, 22 December 1865, AMAA.

[21] E. M. Cravath to Samuel Hunt, 15 December 1865, AMAA; Hiram Eddy to M. E. Strieby, 22 December 1865, AMAA.

available to them, most were forced to live in primitive outbuildings, in indisputably unsanitary conditions.[22]

Nearly 5,000 of Macon's Negro citizens had died by the time the outbreak peaked in the summer of 1866. Alan Conway, in *Reconstruction in Georgia*, stated that coffins were in such great demand that one carpenter needed four assistants to complete his orders.[23]

Obviously, the smallpox outbreak affected freedmen's education in Macon. The night schools were the most severely affected, and in January 1866, shortly after the outbreak, some were forced to close down temporarily. Day school growth, too, was stalled in January, and the AMA saw enrollments decrease quickly.[24]

In spite of the setbacks caused by the smallpox epidemic, the freedmen schools at Macon were officially established by the beginning of 1866. Unfortunately, all Negro teachers who had previously worked for the Freedmen's Bureau had been replaced by white teachers or had been reassigned as their assistants in the evening schools. Even with advancement slowed by the smallpox epidemic and a lack of suitable buildings, Rev. Eddy still could write, "I never knew so much progress made in so short a time. The advance is so marked that I can readily detect it as I pass among the schools from day to day."[25]

When Superintendent Eddy opened night schools on 2 January 1866, the day schools were reduced to one session—either morning or afternoon. "The young ladies cannot work nine hours. It is too much to ask of my teachers," wrote Eddy. Nevertheless, the schools continued to improve. According to Rev. Eddy, "chaos is rising into order," and "our schools are moving forward with usual

---

[22] Alan Conway, *The Reconstruction of Georgia* (Minneapolis: University of Minnesota Press, 1966) 67–68. See especially the *Macon Daily Telegraph* for 17 February and 5, 12, 13, 19, 20, 25, 26 July 1866.

[23] Conway, *Reconstruction in Georgia*, 68.

[24] Teacher Monthly Reports, January and February 1866, AMAA.

[25] Teacher Monthly Reports for January; Hiram Eddy to Samuel Hunt, 1 January 1866, AMAA.

regularity, the interest deepening and extending." By January,
enrollment for day schools numbered well over 700, while night
school attendance grew to more than 200. AMA officials expected
even higher figures as weather conditions improved.[26]

The growing demands of the schools made it difficult for Rev.
Eddy to find time for his regular duties as a missionary at large. He
therefore requested that a male teacher be sent to superintend the
Macon schools, thus freeing him for the missionary work. John
Rockwell arrived from Nashville on 13 January, and four days later
took charge of the AMA schools in Macon. Eddy seemed pleased
with Rockwell and informed AMA officials that "he seems to be the
man. But his coming may not relieve me for the work requires all
our hands every week." In fact, enrollment was more than 1,000,
and Eddy expected a large increase. "But if it will do," he added, "I
shall commence my missionary work next week." Eddy also
appealed for four additional teachers to relieve the strain on
personnel at Macon.[27]

Once in charge, Rockwell, a native of Norwich, Connecticut,
and a Yale University graduate, took some preliminary steps
toward establishing grades in the schools. "Many of our teachers
have not been much used to that style of schools and the colored
people of course [are] unfamiliar with anything of the kind and we
are moving more deliberate than we otherwise should." He took
advanced pupils from the various schools and created a graded
system with high school and a grammar school. Rockwell
converted the various independent schools within each church
building into one school, making one teacher "responsible for the
advancement of the pupils in her school, with the other teacher or
teachers as her assistant or assistants."[28]

---

[26] Hiram Eddy to M. E. Strieby, 1 January 1866, AMAA.

[27] Hiram Eddy to M. E. Strieby, 9 January 1866 and 14 January 1866,
AMAA; John Rockwell to Samuel Hunt, 2 February 1866, AMAA; Hiram Eddy to
M. E. Strieby, 16 January 1866 and 18 January 1866, AMAA.

[28] John Rockwell to Samuel Hunt, 2 February 1866, AMAA.

Rockwell was aware of the continued presence of smallpox and noted that "care is [being] taken to secure our schools from being interrupted by the spread of the disease." To protect teachers and other students, those who had contracted smallpox or who had a family member with the disease were temporarily excluded from school. This precautionary measure was taken "after consultation with some of the leading men of the city, white and colored." Apparently, the policy was successful, as none of the teachers contracted the deadly disease. There were no interruptions in the day schools as a result of the spreading illness. However, night school, which by February had grown to include as many as 340 students, was again suspended for ten days. Moreover, with such a large number of students, "teachers began to break down, and it became necessary to limit the night school to two hundred students."[29]

When smallpox continued to ravage the community, the Freedmen's Bureau intervened. On 16 February, E. G. Locke and Louis J. Lambert of the Freedmen's Bureau issued Special Order No. 7, affecting the freedmen schools:

> As a precautionary measure against the increase of the epidemic raging in our midst, it is ordered that "no pupils shall hereafter be admitted or retained in the schools for freedmen in this town unless they can produce a certificate of vaccination from the city health officer, or some duly qualified practitioner."
>
> Vaccination "gratis" can be had on application to the city health officer.

---

[29] Ibid.; Teacher Monthly Reports, Lincoln Night School, 18 February 1866, AMAA.

Teachers are requested to report to this office within seven days from this date, their receipt, and compliance with this order.[30]

Another problem that continued to plague both the day and night schools was the lack of sufficient funding. The number of students grew so rapidly that both schools were desperately short of "matter to illustrate the subject treated." The $554.20 allocated for January expenses was to pay teachers' salaries and expenses of the teachers' "Home," leaving little to supply the classrooms with needed materials such as maps and globes to aid in teaching geography.[31]

Continually expanding enrollments led Rockwell to request additional first-rate teachers. On 7 February, he made a desperate plea to AMA headquarters:

We are aware that it is somewhat late in the season to send teachers to a distant field. Our wants are however pressing and a thoroughly competent executive woman would be a great value. Should the matter of outgoing travelling expenses be the only objection to her appointment, if need be I will pay fifty dollars toward her travelling expenses here.... I will do the same if need be in regard to a second first class teacher.... Besides laying here the foundation for a large and more extensive work the next season, we hope to accomplish much this year and be permitted to open one or more attraction points near us. Dr. Eddy has found such a place at Milledgeville which in his judgement the association should not fail to occupy.

---

[30] *Macon Daily Telegraph*, 17 February 1866. Locke's role with the Freedmen's Bureau is not clear; he was probably an education official associated with Eberhart.

[31] Bill of Expenses at Macon House for month of January 1866, AMAA.

The need for additional teachers in Macon was in part due to the rush to open a new facility in Milledgeville. "We open at Milledgeville with a part of our force here, and hope to have some relief by the arrival of new teachers. As it seemed best to open this year."[32]

With the arrival of more support staff and the growing experience of the original corps of teachers, the mission schools seemed well on their way to supplying the needs of blacks in Central Georgia. Reception was generally positive, as evidenced in the following article in the *Macon Daily Telegraph* on 7 February 1866.

> More than four thousand colored people of both sexes and all ages are enjoying the privilege of instruction in the schools in this city established since the advent of peace by the charitable people of the North.... There are four morning schools, one in each of the four African Churches; there is one afternoon school, embracing the more advanced pupils of the morning schools; and there is one night school where freedmen of every color, size, age, of both sexes, meet to learn. In the morning schools, which indeed may be denoted a mixed school for from old men of seventy down to the mere child, and from the old married dame to the sprightly yellow lass, all sizes and ages may be seen here.[33]

Freedmen's Bureau Commissioner Oliver O. Howard and other officials considered freedmen education an important priority, and the bureau continued its support when the AMA took charge of the Macon schools. In the fall of 1865, Superintendent Eberhart had toured Georgia towns considered to be sufficiently

---

[32] John Rockwell to Samuel Hunt, 2 February 1866 and 7 February 1866, AMAA; John Rockwell to M. E. Strieby, 10 February 1866, AMAA.

[33] *Macon Daily Telegraph*, 7 February 1866; quoted in Brownlee, *New Day Ascending*, 138; also reprinted in *20th Annual Report of the AMA*, 1866, 31.

populated by African Americans to warrant schools. In his first semi-annual report, John W. Alvord, Inspector of Schools and Finances, reported that the best Georgia schools were in urban areas, including Augusta, Macon, Columbus, Atlanta, and Savannah. From the beginning, Macon was considered a focal point for freedmen education, and both the AMA and the Bureau were determined to provide the necessary means to establish a first-rate educational system there. An important Bureau contribution to freedmen education was Superintendent Eberhart's effort to provide uniform textbooks for the schools throughout Georgia.[34]

The AMA generally used texts from the American Tract Society in its early freedmen's schools. The Teachers Monthly School Reports, after the arrival of the AMA in Macon, clearly show that instruction was taken from the Society's National Series, *The Freedman's Spelling Book*, *The Freedman's Primer*, *The Freedman's Second Reader*, and *The Freedman's Third Reader*. These readers were intended to "impart instruction in matters of history and morality as well as reading" and to "supply the Freedmen with religious truth, biographies of colored persons, religious subjects and from the Word of God."[35]

The monthly report of Lincoln School No. 1, taught by Kate S. Mattison, Eliza Miller, and Emeline S. Kidd, illustrated the content of instruction in an AMA school in Macon. Enrollment at their school totalled 220, with eighty-two males and 138 females. (A pupil was not considered to be enrolled until after five days of attendance.) None of the pupils had progressed beyond *The*

[34] Jones, *Soldiers of Light and Love*, 89–92; and George L. Eberhart, Superintendent Report, 8 October 1866, BRFAL-Ed. Ga.; John W. Alvord, *Inspector's Report of Schools and Finances*, U.S. Bureau of Refugees, Freedmen and Abandoned Lands (Washington, D.C.: U.S. Government Printing Office, 1866–1870); hereafter cited First-Tenth. *First Semi-annual Report*, 1 January 1866.

[35] Robert C. Morris, Introduction to *Freedmen's School and Textbooks* (New York: AMS Press, 1980); also Robert C. Morris, Chapter 5 in *Reading, 'Riting and Reconstruction: The Education of Freedmen in the South* (Chicago: University of Chicago Press, 1976).

Freedman's Primer. The entire school engaged in "oral" and "mental" arithmetic from *Davies Arithmetic,* while 130 took lessons in writing and still others studied from *Cornell's Geography.* The school held classes twenty-one days each month. Some classes took lessons from *Willson's Reader,* which Freedmen's Bureau Commissioner Oliver Otis Howard called "an excellent series [that] has been received and examined with great interest. I like the works very much, and I am especially pleased with the Charts and Primary Books, believing them unusually adapted to aid the child in making a start."[36]

In addition to the texts used in the freedmen schools, the AMA distributed copies of both the *Freedman* and *Freedmen's Journal* to all its teachers in the field. These two journals were intended to "promote educational and religious work among the freed people in Macon." AMA secretary George Whipple instructed Rev. Eddy to "place copies of each in the hands of every teacher under your care, retaining some for yourself" and to "report with the least practicable delay," on their usefulness. Whipple told Eddy that the Boston Tract Society "will furnish them to us at half-price, we will furnish them to you and the teachers free."[37]

By 1 May, Superintendent Rockwell reported that student enrollment in the Macon schools had reached 1,027, with a daily average attendance of 627. The lower average was because of "a number of our scholars having left school to enter service—many out of town." He further reported that "nothing has been done toward night instruction, and the regular sessions have been from 8 till 1 o'clock each day for the four morning schools nos. 1, 2, 3, and 4." The afternoon schools, numbers 5 and 6, held sessions from 2 to 5 p.m. The arrangement for afternoon schools is "by necessity

---

[36] Teachers Monthly School Reports, 30 April 1866; Gen. O. O. Howard, Freedmen's Bureau Commissioner, quoted in *Loyal Georgian,* 6 July 1867, BRFAL-Ed. Ga.

[37] George Whipple to Hiram Eddy, 9 February 1866, John Rockwell papers, AMAA.

not choice, as we are using the four churches and have obtained no other accommodations."[38]

Table 1 summarizes the enrollments for all the Lincoln Free Schools in Macon, showing the teachers at each.

TABLE 1

Abstract of Teachers and Superintendents
for Lincoln Free Schools
Month Ending 31 May 1866*

	Boys	Girls	Total	Average	Teachers
No. 1	94	156	250	165	Mattison, Miller, Kidd
No. 2	32	59	91	69	D. M. Day
No. 3	64	120	184	143	Wells, Stratton
No. 4	39	54	93	58	Glezen, Bridgman
No. 5	93	165	258	153	M. L. Root
No. 6	62	89	151	71	E. M. Miller, Mr. &
	384	643	1027	659	Mrs. E. A. Barnes[39]

The AMA had eleven teachers and several staff stationed in Macon, one of whom, Macon resident Emeline Kidd, was a Southerner by birth. The others hailed from Northern states—two from Illinois, one from Wisconsin, one from Michigan, four from Ohio, two from New York, one from Illinois, and one from Connecticut. Thus, seven states represented the AMA cause in Macon.[40]

---

[38] John Rockwell to G. L. Eberhart, 1 June 1866, Teachers Monthly School Reports, BRFAL-Ed. Ga.

[39] John A. Rockwell, Superintendent's Report, 1 June 1866.

[40] John A. Rockwell, Superintendent Report for Central Georgia, 1 June 1866. According to Swint, *The Northern Teacher in the South*, Appendix III, 175–200, some of the Macon teachers and their hometowns are as follows: Emeline Kidd, Macon; Delia M. Day, Sheffield, Ohio; Elmira Stratton,

As the school term drew to a close, Rockwell reported on what he perceived to be the public sentiments regarding the AMA's mission in Macon:

> We knew little of the real feeling of the community regarding our work. If we can judge by having never been interrupted or interfered with in our work [except] by a few visits from the white citizens, and an occasional expressed approval of our enterprise, we should say that in theory they are favorable to the education of the freedmen but had we not been here would or could hardly have put in practice their theory, a desire to see the freedman improve and become a good member of society, yet taking a different view from us of what he should aspire to become.[41]

The end of the first year of freedmen education was celebrated with joint closing exercises for all the freedmen schools. As described in the *Macon Daily Telegraph*, Superintendent Rockwell opened the ceremony, delivering a "few remarks relative to the progress of the school." Next were declarations of prayer by Mary Porter, Charlie Clayton, and Warren Bohrs "interspersed with singing." Teacher E. A. Barnes made a brief statement "expressing disappointment that more progress had not been made by the scholars." He urged that the students not regress but hold fast to their books during the summer vacation and recommended that (at the expense of four dollars) they attend a "pay school," under the auspices of the Presbyterian church, for six weeks. William Scarborough, a student who later attained fame as a scholar and an

---

Unionville, Ohio; Martha D. Ayers (matron), Worcester, Massachusetts; Rev. Mr. and Mrs. E. A. Barnes, Bakerfield, Connecticut; Sarah M. Wells, Tecumseh, Michigan; Kate Mattison, Mt. Vernon, Ohio. No hometowns are mentioned for Sara L. Glezen, Emma Bridgman, Eliza Miller, or M. L. Root.

[41] John A. Rockwell, Superintendent Report for Central Georgia, 1 June 1866.

educator, was called upon next. "By bad taste or worse selection, his subject was Tennyson's 'Charge of the Light Brigade,' which was about as fit for the occasion as a pig for the parlor," reported the *Telegraph*. Afro-Maconite Robert Bonner followed with words of appreciation and gratification. Jefferson Long, an African American who later served as a U.S. congressman from Georgia, "made by far the best speech of the occasion in our estimation." Long was critical of the lack of "respect to teachers and scholars" exhibited by parents who were not present in the presupposed number. "He indulged in a few rhapsodies of freedom, for which we suppose, he might well be excused," continued the *Telegraph* editor. The program closed with a statement by a leading black Maconite, Lewis Sherman, in which pupils were reminded of the "privileges which had been denied their ancestors during two hundred years of servitude."[42]

All schools taught by the Northern teachers closed 1 July, and were scheduled to reopen early in October, "as is confidently expected, with a largely increased corps of efficient instructors." For students who wanted—and could afford—to continue their schooling through the summer, several pay schools were run under the charge of various AMA officials. Elmira Stratton and several of her colleagues operated a pay school, with proceeds going toward meeting school operational expenses. Stratton's summer school was small, "but thoroughly drilled." Another summer pay school, organized by Eliza Miller at the Freedmen Hospital in Macon, had an enrollment of thirty-seven, with an average attendance of thirty-one. Miller found "good success in instructing the pupils and to some extent improving their condition which was deplorable." Each session at the hospital met for one and a half hours, and Miller was assisted by Elmira Stratton; the two alternated terms.[43]

---

[42] *The Daily Telegraph*, 16 June 1866.

[43] Alvord, *Second Semi-annual Report*, July 1, 1866, 5; Elmira Stratton to W.E. Whiting, 30 June 1866, AMAA; Eliza M. Miller, Teacher Monthly Report, 3 July 1866, AMAA.

The Methodist Church on Walnut Street, too, housed summer school for those students who could pay four dollars. Taught by Mr. and Mrs. E. A. Barnes, with a support staff that included Miller and Stratton, this school enrolled a total of fifty students, with an average attendance of forty-three. E. A. Barnes and company also collected $126 before the end of June to "defray the expenses of the Home."[44]

The 1865–1866 school year had been successful, not only in Macon but across Georgia. In all, according to bureau Superintendent of Education Eberhart, fifty-four schools were organized in the state, with sixty-four teachers and 4,025 scholars; of these, 1,993 had been taught to read by March 1866. Given the limited resources of the Freedmen's Bureau, it became clear that if the freedmen were to have schools, they would have to take on some of the financial burden. In fact, by the end of the first year, nearly $4,000 had been paid by the freedmen themselves to support their schools. During the first year the cornerstone had been laid for the growth and development of black education in the Macon community and Central Georgia for the next seventy-five years. Nevertheless, the course would not be smooth. Opposition from the white community, inadequate facilities, an ongoing struggle for funding, and black poverty caused by unfair labor contracts were some of the factors that would help define the struggle for effective black education in Macon.[45]

---

[44] E.H. Barnes, Superintendent Report, June 1866, AMA.

[45] *The Freedmen Record*, 11 (March 1866): 41; see especially Paul Cimbala, "The Terms of Freedom: The Freedmen's Bureau and Reconstruction in Georgia, 1865–1870" (Ph.D. dissertation, Emory University, 1983), 459.

CHAPTER 2

THE PERIOD OF CONSOLIDATION
1866–1868

In September 1866, en route to Macon, Martha D. Ayers wrote to American Missionary Association headquarters, "I am in the prospect of returning to 'Lincoln Home' [and] Miss [S. M.] Proctor had been commissioned by AMA and comes with me." By October the AMA party had arrived safely in Macon to commence their second school term. No longer complete strangers to the city, the AMA teachers and officials had ceased to be objects of curiosity to the local people and no longer "excited the remarks which last year's debut occasioned." This term, in fact, would mark the start of an eventful two-year period for the AMA in Macon.[1] ✓

After nearly a year in the city, the AMA was committed to extending the effort necessary to create a model school program. For the next few months, much of the AMA official correspondence related to the development of this school system. Although the association continued to use the four schools already established in black churches, additional schools were opened in an

---

[1] Martha D. Ayers to Samuel Hunt, 17 September 1866; Martha D. Ayers to Samuel Hunt, 13 November 1866, American Missionary Association Archives, Amistad Research Center, New Orleans, Louisiana; hereafter cited as AMAA.

outbuilding in the Lincoln Home yard and in a room in the Freedmen's Hospital.[2]

Plans were initiated, with the cooperation of Superintendent Gilbert L. Eberhart of the Freedmen's Bureau, to erect a first-rate school building. Teachers also discussed the possibility of opening a Macon branch of the Freedmen's Savings and Trust Company (called the Freedmen's Bank) to promote self-sufficiency and self-determination among African-American citizens in central Georgia. The AMA's efforts to aid the development of Macon's black community extended to expanding its role in social work activities and securing a Congregational minister and building a new church. Although the AMA faced hindrances from both the white and black communities in instituting its various social and educational programs, by the end of the 1868 school term, the association had realized most of its goals in connection with the Macon field.[3]

Education was only one of the freedmen's needs. AMA missionaries made numerous house calls in and around Macon, providing much needed rations and clothing to the newly liberated citizens. The near failure of the 1866 crops had brought widespread destitution to central Georgia, and many poor freedmen suffered from illness as well as lack of food. During Presidential Reconstruction (1865–1867), many local freedmen fell behind in their rent, and those who sought treatment for illness in their families were likely to find themselves facing inflated doctor bills.[4]

---

[2] G. L. Eberhart to E. P. Smith, 23 February 1867, AMAA; G. L. Eberhart, 8 October 1866, Bureau of Refugees, Freedmen and Abandoned Lands, Educational Division, Georgia (Miscellaneous papers).

[3] Ibid.; Jacqueline Jones, *Soldiers of Light and Love: Northern Teachers and Georgia Blacks, 1865–1873* (Athens: University of Georgia Press, 1992) 161–62.

[4] Julius H. Parmelee, "Freedmen's Aid Societies, 1861–1871," *United States Bureau of Education Bulletin*, No. 38, ed. Thomas Jesse Jones, 282; Teacher Monthly Reports for Emma Bridgman and Maria L. Root, June 1866; Elmira Stratton to William E. Whiting, 30 June 1866, AMAA; *American Missionary* 10 (December 1866): 277; *American Missionary* 12 (March 1868): 52.

Many of the freedmen's problems resulted from the plantation owner's unfair labor practices. Unscrupulous planters turned laborers off their plantations during the winter months after they had finished harvesting the crops. Teacher E. A. Barnes observed that many freedmen who had worked long and diligently "received no pay except their food and perhaps one script of homespun, and sometimes not even that.... When will all these wrongs be righted?" AMA District Superintendent John A. Rockwell wrote AMA officers in New York: "Clothing is now and will always be wanted, but before that can come people are starving." Rockwell ended his letter, "Shall we feed them, or in the name of the American Missionary Association turn a cold shoulder, saying, 'we have nothing for you'— this last we can not do, our visit may best be suspended."[5]

Missionary teachers frequently solicited help from various Northern friends of freedmen, but often the responses were "slow to come," and many letters never generated, or "called out" a response. In the face of widespread poverty and deprivation, Martha Ayers, who served as matron of the "Home," often drew upon her own "small salary to above one half of that due her for the month" to help those in need.[6]

Ayers frequently visited the "lowly," and on one occasion observed a mother lying still beside her wailing baby, without any cover and in an open building. "The mother's bosom is bare as though her last conscious act had been an effort to nurse her child." Ayers learned that for several days the woman had eaten only a "morsel of bread" and that her sick husband, Lot, had left home a few hours earlier to beg for food. Ayers described in the *American Missionary* how she "waited for a time, hoping he (Lot)

---

[5] *American Missionary* 12 (March 1868): 52; Martha D. Ayers and John A. Rockwell to American Missionary Headquarters, New York, 31 October 1866, AMAA; *American Missionary* 10 (December 1866): 277.

[6] Martha D. Ayers to Samuel Hunt, 13 November 1866; Martha D. Ayers and John A. Rockwell to George Whipple, 31 October 1866, AMAA; *American Missionary* 10 (December 1866): 277.

will come, but he does not, and I leave the mother and the child alone."[7]

A frustrated Ayers also reported on the dreadful circumstances facing the Morton family. Knocking at the door of their crude shelter, she was welcomed by a "feeble voice." Inside, she found Henry Morton sitting near a fireless hearth, suffering from smallpox. For five weeks Morton's illness had prevented him from working and thus from obtaining adequate food. He had eaten no breakfast and only one meal the day before, and in one corner, "upon some filthy ragged bedding," slept a sick child who had eaten only a potato for dinner. Morton, whom she called an "earnest working man," was one of those unable to collect his wages from his employers, and to make matters worse, an agent was threatening to turn the family into the street for overdue rent. With such unyielding conditions, Ayers wrote, "I hope the offspring of freedom has not died out in his soul [although] the wreck of every expectation is visible in his face." Another worker in the field asked, "What am I to do in view of the actual hunger, starvation and wretchedness, which opens to my view with each opening door?"[8]

Other teachers had similar concerns about the deplorable conditions facing Macon's poor black population. Wrote one Macon teacher, "My heart aches as I go among them and see such destitution and suffering, and feel my utter powerlessness to supply their needs from our limited resources." On occasion, the missionaries' prayers were answered with boxes and barrels of clothing, socks, blankets, and other much needed items. And for members of the black community who desired to tend gardens, the AMA offered seeds, which were distributed by local teachers.[9]

---

[7] *American Missionary* 10 (February 1866): 276.

[8] Ibid., 277–78.

[9] *American Missionary* 12 (March 1868): 52–53; J. C. Hathaway to John A. Rockwell, 9 November 1866, 25 January 1867 and 6 February 1867; E. P. Smith to John A. Rockwell, 6 March 1867, John A. Rockwell papers, AMAA.

AMA officials generally preferred women, whom they called "laborers," for its Southern mission fields. "Where the work and want are greatest, women must be largely the workers." AMA policy held that the "dexterous hand of woman" was best equipped to supply the necessities of freedmen. "Our girls have had more time and leisure to pursue their studies,... Their superiors in education, refinement, and purpose to do good cannot be found the world over." A few years later, an AMA publication setting out its program for women in the field, stated that "woman can go like a princess into these cabins, carry and cook the food, bear and administer the medicine, offer the fuel and the clothing; and with soft and gentle hand, perform all the little, nameless acts and ministries that soothe the sick and comfort the dying." That women could be paid smaller salaries than men no doubt was another factor in the AMA's sending a preponderance of women teachers to the South.[10]

Northern white teachers were not popular with white Southerners. Most Macon whites were not enthusiastic about black education and looked with disdain upon the teachers' visits to freedmen's homes and churches. Nevertheless, the AMA fared better in Macon than in some other Georgia cities, where in 1866 whites had burned down several buildings, including a church used for a freedmen school. Indeed, by mid-1867, Freedmen's Bureau School Inspector John W. Alvord reported that opposition to black education appeared to have lessened in Macon and that no physical obstruction had occurred, noting "a most wonderful change in regard to the education of the colored race within the last five months." Referring to the situation at Macon and some other areas of Georgia, Freedmen's Bureau Superintendent Eberhart commented on the "revolution in the hearts and minds of rebels as never was seen before. No more 'nigger,' 'our colored population' now! no disgrace now for whites to attend nigger meetings—I

---

[10] American Missionary Association, *Woman's Work for the Lowly* (Boston: South Inquirer Press, 1873) 7.

mean colored meetings." As will be seen, Alvord and Eberhart underestimated white hostility to black education.[11]

The Southern press, too, had softened its opposition toward freedmen education by 1867. "Many newspapers have suddenly discovered that since there is no disgrace or loss of caste in teaching Africans in the missionary fields, there should be none in teaching the [N]egro here at home," Alvord contended. Still, many whites who accepted education for freedmen thought the teachers should be from the South. In 1866 Bishop Elliott of Georgia wrote in the Southern journal *DeBow's Review*, "Every person imported from abroad to instruct or teach these people is an influence, unintentionally perhaps, but really, widening the breach between the races. This work must be done by ourselves." White Southerners still feared the Northern influence on the freedmen. The number of "preachers, doctors, white men and women—within the last month continually besieging me for employment" in the black schools amazed Eberhart. It was unclear whether the applicants were motivated by a need for jobs and money, a desire to keep Northerners out of black schools, or by a genuine concern for freedmen education. Alvord thought that these white Southerners, if they could "assimilate" to the work, could perhaps "disarm surrounding prejudice, and if not already qualified, may, by practice, become acceptable if not proficient in the art of teaching."[12]

By fall 1866 the Macon schools were reasonably well staffed, although poor physical conditions and facilities continued to present problems. That October, in anticipation of the coming

---

[11] John W. Alvord, *Inspector's Report of Schools and Finances*, U.S. Bureau of Refugees, Freedmen and Abandoned Lands (Washington, D.C.: U.S. Government Printing Office, 1866–1870); hereafter cited First-Tenth. *Third Semi-annual Report*, 1 January 1867, 16; Alvord, *Fourth Semi-annual Report*, 1 July 1867, 34; Gilbert L. Eberhart to E. P. Smith, 8 April 1867, AMAA.

[12] Alvord, *Fourth Semi-annual Report*, 1 July 1867, 17; *DeBow's Review*, Volume II (After the War Series), New Orleans, 1866, 313; "Abroad" here refers to the North; Gilbert L. Eberhart to E. P. Smith, 8 April 1867, AMAA; Alvord, *Third Semi-annual Report*, 1 January 1867, 37.

winter, Superintendent Rockwell appealed for "old fashioned Franklin" stoves both for Macon's mission 'Home" and for nearby Milledgeville. School closings due to extreme weather were common, and in January 1867 Eugene Upton and Eliza Miller reported that they were forced to close Lincoln Free School number 1 for several days because of a "cold school room."[13]

In light of such events, the AMA was delighted when, on 23 February 1867, Superintendent Eberhart proposed that the Bureau provide, at its own expense, a new school building for Macon. Eberhart's primary reason for desiring a permanent building was to enable the AMA to provide a normal program to train black teachers for central Georgia. "With the Bible, spelling-book, and freedom as the basis of instruction, the poorest teaching is far better than the present ignorance, and the South must ultimately do the whole of this work," wrote Alvord. Officials acknowledged the need for black teachers, "even when inferior in qualification," to extend education into the rural and plantation districts where many were already employed.[14]

In the meantime, in order to supplement its limited funds, the AMA introduced a tuition requirement at the start of the 1866–1867 school year. It soon discovered that many families were unable to pay even a small amount and enrollments plummeted, dropping in October to 320. While the AMA claimed that each teacher instructed as many pupils as could "be advantageously taught," the tuition system was abandoned quietly in early December after Macon blacks pledged to raise $1,500. The effect was immediate, and enrollment jumped to 448 students. The completion of the cotton harvest probably contributed to the increase as well.[15]

---

[13] John A. Rockwell to William E. Whiting, 11 October 1866, AMAA; Eliza Miller and Eugene Upton, Teacher Monthly Report, January 1867, AMAA.

[14] Gilbert L. Eberhart to E. P. Smith, 23 February 1867, AMAA; Alvord, *Third Semi-annual Report*, 1 January 1867, 15, 16.

[15] Martha D. Ayers to Samuel Hunt, 22 September 1866, John A. Rockwell Papers, AMAA; Martha D. Ayers to Samuel Hunt, 13 November 1866; John A. Rockwell, Superintendent Reports for Macon, November and December 1866,

After crops were harvested, more adults were able to attend classes, and in November 1866, on Alvord's recommendation, AMA teachers in Macon added classes in moral training for adult students in the night school. He "urged that adults be brought as possible, into night and Sabbath schools" to be taught "true manhood." This could be done, he said, "to a very great extent, if not solely, by oral instruction." Alvord preferred teaching the precepts of "the commandments, the Lord's Prayer, the Beatitudes, and many other portions of the Scriptures." Regular academic instruction for adult students included reciting the capital cities, U.S. territories, principal rivers and mountains, and history linked with early America. The night sessions continued throughout 1867, with enrollment climbing to as many as 519 pupils.[16]

The 1867–1868 school year opened with five schools, the four Lincoln Free schools and a grammar school, under the joint operation of the AMA and the Freedmen's Bureau. There were nine teachers. Schools 1 and 3 operated as primary schools, 2 and 4 as secondary. The fifth, a grammar school, for students who had progressed beyond the early readers and mastered basic skills, opened first on 17 October, followed by the primary and secondary schools on 28 October. Members of a delegation from the *Loyal Georgian* who visited two of the Macon schools were impressed with J. A. Rockwell, calling him "one of the most efficient school superintendents we have ever known." The delegation also found the students impressive as they performed a written exercise involving the use of slates: "A lesson [was] given out by the teacher, and the skill displayed by these little boys and girls was

AMAA; for an example of the effect of an agrarian economy on school attendance see S. L. Smith, "The Relation of Farm Labor to School Terms and Attendance" (Master's thesis, George Peabody College for Teachers, 1918).

[16] Alvord, *Third Semi-annual Report*, 1 January 1867, 15–16; John A. Rockwell, Superintendent Reports, November and December 1866; Mary C. Day, Polly Gardner, Jennie McConnell, Eliza Miller, S. M. Proctor, Elmira Stratton, and Eugene Upton, Teacher Monthly Reports, January 1867, AMAA.

astonishing" and "showed clearly that the instruction had been thorough."[17]

AMA schools suffered a temporary decline in enrollment in fall of 1867. Teachers reported "that several tuition schools, mostly under the management of colored teachers, had sprang up before and during the last vacation; and some of our former scholars were attending these schools." Many of the older students were working on the fall harvest; others were unable to attend or were "detained by sickness."[18]

Despite lower enrollments the AMA teachers returned in the fall of 1867 to greatly improved accommodations. A new mission "Home" was located in "a more convenient and healthy part of the city." Frank Haley described the new "Home" as "pleasant...very plainly furnished...yet comfortable and I think we are all very happy in it."[19]

Haley and his wife, recent AMA appointees from Wolfboro, New Hampshire, arrived to tend to religious affairs in Macon and surrounding counties. He found

> everything connected with this post different from and better than we had expected. It did not require many days to show us that the work here had been systematized to a degree altogether unanticipated and good results had already been largely achieved.... One cannot stand before these schools for the first, second, third or hundredth time without profound astonishment at what has been already accomplished.

---

[17] Frank Haley to E. P. Smith, 1 December 1867, AMAA; *American Missionary* 11 (September 1867): 209.

[18] *American Missionary* 11 (September 1867): 209.

[19] Ibid.

He also was pleased to report his finding of "bright intelligent faces, beaming eyes, quick responses, and earnest attention and the great teachers."[20]

Haley regarded the grammar school, "one of the most interesting schools I have ever seen," to be a fair representation of the AMA's labor in Macon: "Its grade of scholarship is high, its discipline is excellent while an unusual degree of earnestness and effectiveness characterize all exercises." He noted that "a part of the time last season it was housed in a windowless barn," but accommodations had improved. Haley was pleased to report that as of December 1867 grammar school enrollment numbered more than one hundred and enrollment for night school, which was taught in a grammar school room and at the "Home," had reached 120. Too, large increases were expected after the Christmas holidays. Haley closed by saying, "This is a most joyous part of our work. It is unmixed delight to teach these men and women."[21]

Haley's primary mission was to tend to religious affairs in the Macon area. Although he thought more effort was needed in that direction, he admitted that "there is evidently much being done, in a quiet way for Christ." He planned "to organize a Sabbath School out of the hundreds of children which are in no way connected with Sabbath Schools of colored churches." Although it was "a slow hard, perplexing work,...by the grace of God we hope to make the attempt," wrote Haley.[22] His effort was rewarded when in spring of 1868, 868 people of all ages gathered at a Baptist church to attend a Sabbath School concert. There were "not a few aged black men and women among those who made recitations of Scripture texts, and as the sacred words came from their untutored memories and trembling lips, they sank with a new power upon the souls of many

---

[20] Ibid.
[21] Frank Haley to E. P. Smith, 1 December 1867, AMAA.
[22] Ibid.

present, who from the depths of grateful hearts whispered the ejaculation, thank God."[23]

In March 1868 the new school constructed by the Bureau opened, and with it a new era of normal school instruction for blacks in Macon. The new building was named Lewis High School after General John R. Lewis, director of the Freedmen's Bureau in Georgia. The *American Missionary* of June 1868 and the annual report described the new facility as located on a "sightly lot" and in every respect a most "commodious and well furnished building." The opening of Lewis High enabled the AMA to provide a "model training school for colored teachers in the South." Up until this moment, AMA schools in Macon had been conducted in church rooms that were "imperfectly heated and without proper school seats." The AMA was proud of the many pupils who had made tremendous progress in spite of the conditions. Now, the Macon teachers "carried their pupils rapidly forward in their studies, preparing them for their seats in the new school building" and for a graded school system.[24]

On 26 March 1868 leading members of both races attended the dedication of the new school. The program opened with a prayer, singing, and a historical sketch of the school's origin. Edmund Asa Ware, AMA's superintendent for "colored" education in Georgia and head of Atlanta University, was the main speaker. He was followed by General Lewis, who was mild mannered and "to the point and acknowledged the compliment of the school's being named after him." The program closed with remarks by future African-American congressman Jefferson Long. He urged the crowd to assemble in front of the chapel on the street to give three cheers to the American flag, "thus clearly showing," stated the *Georgia Weekly Telegraph* editor, "that he could not let a purely

---

[23] *American Missionary* 12 (June 1868): 122; *22nd Annual Report of the AMA*, 1868, 44–45.

[24] *American Missionary* 12 (June 1868): 122–23; *22nd Annual Report of the AMA*, 1868, 44–45.

local matter proceed in its regular routine, without lugging in the chance to make political capital."[25]

The dedication was not without its tense moments. Some of the local white guests were unhappy with Ware's oration. As Southerners, they were enraged by what Ware "spit out and could not digest the bitter untruths he promulgated." Two white pastors, E. W. Warren and David Wills, informed the *Telegraph* of their dissatisfaction with Ware's speech: "From the high and responsible position he holds, we were almost prepared to expect a flow of reason and at least of soul," they wrote, but Ware, completely disregarding protocol, "introduced his speech with a bitter tirade against the South." Considering the speech as "nothing but low appeal to the vulgar prejudices of the crowd," both pastors "instantly rose and, with a feeling of indignation, left the hall."[26]

Echoing and expanding upon Bishop Elliott's earlier statement, the *Telegraph* stated that Ware's performance had "fully persuaded" the white citizens of Macon "that there can never exist any true peace and harmony between the two races so long as the political preachers and pseudo philanthropists of the North have control of the educational and religious interest of the freedmen." The *Telegraph* concluded its remarks by asserting, first, that "our people cannot co-operate with this class of teachers" in any united fashion, and second, if the head of freedmen education for Macon wished Christian gentlemen to attend "their public exercises they must engage none but Christian gentlemen to deliver addresses on such occasions."[27]

The June 1868 *American Missionary* responded to the *Telegraph*'s criticism, calling Ware's address "clear and forcible, and with the exception of but one sentence could not have been objected to by even these reverenced champions of secession and rebellion." The association claimed the right to "unrestricted

---

[25] "The Dedication of Lewis High School" and "Protest," *Georgia Weekly Telegraph*, 3 April 1868.

[26] "Protest," *Georgia Weekly Telegraph*, 3 April 1868.

[27] Ibid.

utterance" of Northern sentiments and "privilege to speak the convictions of mind and heart." Despite certain philosophical differences with some local whites on the nature of freedmen education, the AMA was pleased with its new school.[28]

Lewis High School opened in March 1868 with an enrollment of 809. About half the students were instructed in eight large school rooms accommodating fifty students each. Another one hundred pupils formed an ungraded class, and the remaining students constituted a subprimary school, which was held each afternoon in the adjoining, newly built Norwich Chapel. The subprimary classes were taught by normal students being prepared as teachers. The normal class "consisted of a dozen masters and misses gathered from among the most advanced and promising pupils in the various schools in this district." These students were given special instruction in the art of teaching and were required to observe the model primary school. In the afternoons, they practiced the art of teaching.[29]

Georgia's freedmen schools, though still few in number, had improved greatly by 1868, and not just in Macon. Thanks to the "improved facilities in the erection of the new buildings," Alvord wrote, "and more improved methods of study…schools in Georgia [are] as good as any in the United States, for the time they have been organized." To his superiors in the AMA, Rockwell wrote,

> In our higher grades much attention has been given to practical arithmetic, intellectual arithmetic and map drawing on the blackboard on the plan of professor Guyot in his intermediate geography, which geography I esteem invaluable as a textbook for advanced classes. In our most advanced school besides the usual third reader, intermediate geography, intellectual and practical arithmetic, spelling exercises, oral and written, and grammar, we have one young man studying

---

[28] *American Missionary* 12 (June 1868): 124.
[29] Alvord, *Seventh Semi-annual Report,* 15.

Latin and Algebra, besides a small class in Harkness's *First Latin Book.*[30]

Writing in the *American Missionary*, one Northern clergyman praised the "teachers [at Macon] who can not be surpassed by any in New England." He described "intelligent, refined, thoroughly capable" teachers who brought into the classroom "the latest and best method of imparting instruction in vogue in the common schools of Boston and Worcester."[31]

Based on testimonies, letters of recommendation, and their prior training and experience, Macon's missionary teachers were indeed well equipped for the task of imparting "the latest and best method" to their black students. Of the approximately three dozen teachers in the AMA's Macon schools from 1866 to 1870, only two were white Southerners. Twenty-five hailed from New England: from Massachusetts (ten), Connecticut (nine), Vermont (three), New Hampshire (two), and Maine (one). One each came from the Mid-Atlantic states of New Jersey and New York. Seven were from the Midwest: from Ohio (four), Illinois (two), and Michigan (one). During this period only three males were employed by the AMA in Macon: Rockwell, Haley, and teacher Eugene Upton.[32]

As a group, the Northern teachers who went South to labor among the destitute freedmen were enthusiastic, benevolent, and professional. Their tenure tended to be short, however. Each year the AMA supported around sixteen teachers in Macon. They remained on average two to three years; only four who were present in 1866 were still there in 1870.[33]

Those who sought commissions as freedmen teachers generally presented letters on their behalf from their ministers. For example,

---

[30] John A. Rockwell to American Missionary Headquarters, 1868, n.d., AMAA.

[31] *22nd Annual Report of the AMA*, 1868, 45.

[32] See *21st Annual Report of the AMA* and *22nd Annual Report of the AMA*, 1867 and 1868, respectively, for list of teachers.

[33] Ibid.; Jones, *Soldiers of Light and Love*, 39–41.

Rev. A. R. Rees, Rector of Christ Church in Macon, wrote to AMA officials commending Emeline Kidd "as a capable teacher and worthy member of the church." Kidd, a local white resident, had begun teaching freedmen in Macon prior to the AMA presence there.[34]

A letter of recommendation for Elizabeth Barnes described her as a person whose "missionary spirit" could not be questioned as "the work...has long lain near her heart." Miss Barnes's "advantages and social connections have been of the first order" fitting her "for any position in life," wrote G. F. Wright in her behalf. Wright also mentioned that although in general she enjoyed good health she was susceptible to severe colds in the harsh winters of Bakersfield, Vermont. Other supporters portrayed her as "thoroughly educated of a decidedly practical turn." Barnes previously had taught in AMA schools in Norfolk, Virginia.[35]

Esther Terry came to Macon with a variety of experiences, including having served as a nurse for the U.S. Medical Department during the Civil War. She later worked for the National Freedmen's Relief Association of the District of Columbia, in Baltimore, and other places, "nursing the wounded sick and dying soldiers and was thankful for the privilege." When AMA Corresponding Secretary Samuel Hunt requested a letter of reference in Terry's favor, several of her superiors, including Foster Freeland and George Lyman, responded. Freeland wrote that Terry embodied all the "requisites of the schedule of your qualifications." Lyman indicated that "since the close of the war she has been

---

[34] See *20th Annual Report of the AMA* and *22nd Annual Report of the AMA*, 1866 and 1868, respectively, for teacher lists; Jacqueline Jones, "Women Who Were More Than Men: Sex and Status in Freedmen's Teaching," *History of Education Quarterly* 19 (Spring 1979): 48–49; A. R. Rees, Testimonial, 23 November 1866, AMAA.

[35] G. F. Wright to George Whipple, 31 January 1866; G. C. Wells to Samuel Hunt, 5 June 1866; E. R. Wells (wife of G. C. Wells) to George Whipple, 5 January 1866, AMAA.

anxious to labor among the freedmen...in spirit of noble self-sacrifice."[36]

In 1867 Catherine Gould joined the missionary "family" at the Lincoln "Home." Gould, a primary teacher who had taught previously in Pennsylvania, was described as being of "high moral character" and "strict integrity." Although, one of her supporters wrote, her "enunciation of words [was] not the most perfect...her scholars always seemed to understand," thus fitting her "for the peculiar duties of teacher of the freedmen." Another "willing teacher," Harriet C. Foote, was described as "gentle and kind in her manners and constantly cheerful." She seemed "eminently fitted" for work as a freedmen teacher "having assisted...satisfactorily in the care of our little ones," wrote Fisk P. Brewer from New Haven. Having obtained appropriate letters of recommendation to "teach among the contrabands," Foote began her work in Macon in 1868.[37]

Mary E. Smith of New London, Connecticut, was commissioned with no teaching experience, although apparently she had gained some by the time she arrived in Macon in 1868. Mary E. Hart, an accomplished public school teacher in Durham Centre, Connecticut, also arrived in 1868. Ella Roper, from Worcester, Massachusetts, followed in 1869. These well-bred, well-educated, well-meaning women were typical of the teachers hired by the AMA for their schools in Macon.[38]

---

[36] Foster Freeland to Samuel Hunt, 8 February 1866, AMAA; George Lyman to Samuel Hunt, 7 and 9 February 1866; D. L. Dix, Office of Superintendent of Women Nurses, to American Missionary Headquarters, April 1864, AMAA.

[37] Thomas H. Burch and Robert C. Taylor, Testimonials, 29 September 1865; A. Elwain, Testimonial, 5 October 1865, AMAA; William H. Lewis, Testimonial, 10 June 1864; W. Stone and Fisk P. Brewer, Testimonials, 5 July 1864, AMAA.

[38] David C. Camp, Testimonial, 14 February 1864; G. Buckingham to George Whipple, 19 April 1864; Henry P. Haven to George Whipple, 19 April 1864; J. W. Sessions, Testimonial, 14 February 1864; A. C. Pierce, Testimonial, 15 February 1864; Lewis Sabin, Testimonial, 20 October 1863, AMAA.

Although the AMA's primary aim was freedmen education, the association was almost as concerned with blacks' spiritual welfare. Macon's black population was predominantly Baptist, Methodist, and Presbyterian, with a few Catholics. The AMA had hoped to bring some of the people it served into its Congregational Church, and thus impart a different type of religious worship. It would certainly be different from what Rev. Hiram Eddy had witnessed in 1866, a conversion he described as like "when one comes to the light" or has "got thro" into God's kingdom. Eddy reported the "ecstasies expressed in conversion...in the Methodist and Baptist churches, the scene when one gets thro [as] something awful. The excitement is beyond description. Their sense of sin sometimes seems indescribably fearful, and when the burden is lifted, the joy is correspondingly great."[39]

AMA officials admired black religiosity, but with few exceptions considered freedmen ministers as immoral and ignorant and their congregations as loud and emotional. As one teacher said, "The people are a *religious* people...they love to sing and pray and have their shouts, but practical religion they know little of." The AMA sought to free freedmen from "the fetters of superstition and sin" and bring them "into the glorious liberty of the gospel." Unfortunately, "most AMA workers never fathomed the slave's religion which emphasized joy and collective hope" more than "personal guilt and self-denial."[40]

Despite its claim of being nonsectarian, the AMA built Congregational churches in cities where it labored, and such was the case in Macon. A chapel was built adjacent to the new school with funds donated by the Second Congregational Church in Norwich, Connecticut. Named the Norwich Chapel after its benefactors, the structure measured seventy by forty feet and adhered to Gothic architectural style. The interior was "a model of taste and symmetrical beauty"; the outside was white with brown

---

[39] *American Missionary* 10 (May 1866): 113–14.
[40] *American Missionary* 17 (August 1861): 178–79; S. S. Jocelyn to G. Whipple, 20 June 1862, AMAA; Richardson, *Christian Reconstruction*, 143.

trim. The chapel was dedicated on 12 April 1868, only two weeks after the Lewis High ceremony. An audience of 600 overflowed from the chapel into the adjoining school rooms. Reverend Dana, pastor of the Second Congregational Church, came from Norwich to present the dedicatory sermon, and C. F. P. Bancroft of Lookout Mountain, Tennessee, gave a prayer. Dana assured the Macon community that Norwich Chapel was "no political device" but an "emblem of universal liberty" to aid the ignorant, poor and the oppressed." Membership in the church remained relatively small. The AMA was far more successful in education than in proselytizing.[41]

The teachers were wise to look ahead to summer vacation and to begin soliciting money for their travel home. The files are filled with numerous letters from Georgia teachers to AMA headquarters concerning the lack of timely payment—the teachers consistently received their salaries two to three months late. Typical was a 23 May letter from teacher Rhonda Lyon requesting the AMA "to send me money for my travelling expenses from this place to my home in Oberlin, Ohio, in addition...at least one month's salary and two if possible." Few letters captured the essence of the state of affairs as well as a note of the same date from Hannah Grosvenor: "It might be better for the AMA just now if it had fewer poor country ministers' daughters or northern carpetbaggers among its teachers." She lamented that "the classes are not supplied with bank stock U. S. Bonds or independent friends who have a store of cash constantly on hand from which supplies can be drawn in cases of emergency." Finally, she apologized for her "departure from the business track, $56 then you will oblige."[42]

---

[41] *American Missionary* 12 (June 1868): 124–25.

[42] Rhonda J. Lyon to W. E. Whiting, 23 May 1868; Hannah H. Grosvenor to W. E. Whiting, 23 May 1868, AMAA.

As the 1867–1868 school year drew to a close, the AMA could boast that in three years in Macon they had taught more than 2,500 of the city's 6,000 African Americans to read and write.[43]

Another important AMA goal also was realized in 1868, when a branch of the Freedmen's Saving and Trust Company was established. The Freedmen's Saving and Trust was chartered in 1865 to teach ex-slaves the importance of "industry and thrift," and the AMA soundly applauded the bank's goals. Since February 1867, Rockwell had sought to bring the bank to Macon. The AMA was confident that freedmen would deposit their money, however small the amounts, in the hope of acquiring savings large enough to obtain a home and land.[44]

The *American Union* of 19 June 1868 reported details of the arrangements: "The Freedpeople of Macon, at the instigation of Mr. H. M. Turner [a state legislator from Macon and a bishop of the African Methodist Episcopal Church], met at the African Methodist Church last Monday night and took the necessary steps for the establishment of a branch bank of the National Freedmen's Saving and Trust Company, in Macon." In the presence of more than 800 people, Turner was named as cashier, Rockwell as president, and fifteen others were selected to serve as members of the bank advisory committee. The *American Union* described the bank's founding "as one of the best moves that could be made at this time, as it will be means of inspiring the colored people with confidence, and turning them into the channel that leads to respectability." With completion of the final arrangements for the Freedmen's Bank, the AMA had made Macon home for the prototype programs it had instituted in only a few select Southern

---

[43]"Review of the School Year Normal Instruction," *American Missionary* 12 (November 1868): 244–45; *22nd Annual Report of the AMA*, 1868, 45.

[44] Carl R. Osthaus, *Freedmen, Philanthropy, and Fraud: A History of the Freedmen's Saving Bank* (Urbana: University of Illinois Press, 1976) 80, 203; John A. Rockwell to E. P. Smith, 6 February 1867, AMAA; *American Missionary* 13 (November 1869): 243–44; Alvord, *Fifth Semi-annual Report*, 1 January 1868, 50; Alvord, *Eighth Semi-annual Report*, 1 July 1869, 87; *American Union*, 19 June 1868.

cities and had consolidated and expanded its role in the life of the black community.[45]

---

[45] *American Union*, 19 June 1868.

CHAPTER 3

LEWIS HIGH SCHOOL
1868–1877

With the opening of the new Lewis High School in the fall of 1868, the American Missionary Association (AMA) set the stage for African-American education in Middle Georgia for the next seventy-four years, and especially for teacher training through normal instruction. Nonetheless, the future was fraught with difficulties. Members of the white community continued to view the AMA presence with ambivalence. The black community in general welcomed the association, but an increasing segment of the black population was moving toward black sovereignty with regard to both education and religion. The AMA began to encounter some difficulty in implementing its various philosophies within Macon's black community. Although the AMA increasingly emphasized building up its religious agenda as an essential component of freedmen instruction, it failed to implant Congregationalism as a viable religion in Macon. An even more perplexing problem the AMA faced during this period was how to ameliorate strained relations with the Bibb County Board of Education when the state began to assume some of the responsibility for universal education. The anxiety created by these conditions split the black community in Macon and created trouble in the otherwise peaceful "Home."

A growing presence of black private and charity schools continued to affect the Lewis High enrollment. When Superintendent Rockwell reported on Lewis High School to the association in December 1868, enrollment had dwindled to 381 students, taught by nine teachers. The following July, John W. Alvord commented on the growth and proliferation of private schools in Georgia, saying that "the better class of freedmen" preferred to send their children to schools that had been organized by local black churches. These schools charged "from fifty cents to one dollar per month," as opposed to the supposedly better-equipped schools run by Northern societies, which never excluded the poor for lack of tuition payments. This was especially true of the AMA schools in larger cities such as Macon, where the association had "excellent white teachers and convenient school-houses." Both the Freedmen's Bureau and the AMA were bewildered by freedmen who sent their children to these schools: "The freedmen will send their children to ignorant colored teachers, occupying uncomfortable school-rooms, and pay them one dollar a month tuition rather than send them to the society schools, and pay fifty or twenty-five cents a month," said one commentary.[1]

Although Macon was a center of AMA support, the AMA never monopolized freedmen education in Macon. A small number of tuition schools were supplanted by the AMA when the association first arrived there in 1865; a few endured, some suspended operations, and others moved to outlying areas to provide education to students outside the city. In 1869 and 1870 at least eleven such schools made official reports to the Freedmen's Bureau Superintendent John R. Lewis. A few, funded irregularly by the Bibb County Board of Education, operated as poor or charity schools, providing education to students unable to pay. Most were supported completely by freedmen and operated in church

---

[1] John Rockwell, Superintendent Report for Macon, December 1868, AMAA; John W. Alvord, *Inspector's Report of Schools and Finances*, U. S. Bureau of Refugees, Freedmen and Abandoned Lands (Washington, D.C.: U.S. Government Printing Office, 1866–1870); hereafter cited First-Tenth; *Seventh Semi-annual Report*, 1 July 1869, 30; *Ninth Semi-annual Report*, 27, 29. It should be noted that the AMA did charge a nominal fee for tuition at Lewis High School.

buildings or in buildings owned by private individuals. These
schools on average enrolled a combined total of 300 to 400 pupils
in any given period during 1869 and 1870 and generally catered to
primary-level students. At least two of these schools provided
industrial education. Despite a growing number of these satellite
schools that siphoned off potential students, Lewis High remained
the choice school for blacks in Macon, as it was the only one that
provided secondary and normal training.[2]

The AMA had always advocated moral education, but with the
opening of Lewis High, even greater emphasis was given to
developing the moral and religious character of the students. AMA
officials taught abstinence by forming temperance societies in its
schools. Alvord wrote that much had been done for the temperance
cause through a new reform organization, called the Vanguard of
Freedom. An auxiliary of the Lincoln Temperance Association, the
Vanguard of Freedom Association was intended to extend its
influence among the children. Members were required to pledge
themselves to abstain from all intoxicating drinks, from the use of
tobacco in any form, and from all profane and vulgar language.[3]

Georgia had no fewer than nine divisions of the Vanguard of
Freedom, with a total of 418 members. Alvord described Macon's
Howard Division as "a very fine and flourishing temperance
organization." Macon teachers frequently reported on division
activities. Vanguard members not only were discouraged from
using strong drink and tobacco but also were strongly encouraged
to avoid objectionable language or speech, including, for example,
the use of "fool," "liar," "thief," and "nigger." The association's

---

[2] See Teacher Monthly School Reports for J. W. Brooks, May 1869 and
March 1870; Belle Hanson, May 1869; Robert U. Mitchell, March 1869; Enoch
Parker, May and June 1869 and January 1870; S. H. Roberson, n.d.; Nathaniel D.
Sneed, January 1870; Lewis Smith, May 1869; Lewis William, 1869; Eli Wilson,
June 1869; and Ariadine Woodliff, May 1869 and January 1870; All in Bureau of
Refugees, Freedmen and Abandoned Lands, Educational Division, Georgia;
hereafter cited as BRFAL-Ed. Ga.

[3] Alvord, *Fourth Semi-annual Report*, 1 July 1867, 89; Alvord, *Sixth Semi-annual Report*, 1 July 1868, 67.

attitude was that intemperance among blacks, as with all its victims, exerted "a baneful influence, especially deleterious to their educational prospects." Alvord wrote, "We do not find them notoriously given to this vice by any means.... These societies are constantly increasing, and are doing much to train their members in all correct moral habits." The AMA sought to inculcate that the "duties to manhood, to home, to country and to God, are immense fields in which to cultivate the virtue of temperance." Obviously, the association was unable to achieve total abstinence, yet, unquestionably, for many, the movement in Macon proved to be beneficial.[4]

After the completion of the Norwich Chapel, Sabbath schooling was intensified. Philip D. Cory, a cashier at the Freedmen Bank in Atlanta who was accused—and acquitted—of embezzling $8,000, served as an AMA teacher and filled in briefly in the pulpit after the departure of the popular minister Frank Haley. Cory found it difficult to sustain a sizable congregation. "We are coming on very well here in some respects, our congregation [is] slowly, but steadily increasing," he wrote, but "members are leaving us, going out after employment...[and] to school." Before Cory withdrew his commission to return to Atlanta, he managed to establish Sabbath schools in outlying areas of Macon using funds obtained from Boston and his own salary.[5]

---

[4] Alvord, *Fourth Semi-annual Report*, 1 July 1867, 89; Alvord, *Fifth Semi-annual Report*, 1 January 1868, 50; Alvord, *Sixth Semi-annual Report*, 1 July 1868; Thomas J. Conaty, *The Temperance Idea in Public Instruction* (Boston: Massachusetts State Teachers' Association, 1894) 8; for list of songs see, American Temperance Union, *Band of Hope Melodies: Adapted to Band of Hope, Cadet, and Other Temperance Meetings* (New York: American Temperance Union, 1860). See also Teacher Monthly Reports for January 1870: Ellen W. Abbott, Helen M. Leonard, Sarah H. Stevens, and Mary E. Hart. It should be noted that the four teachers in January of 1870 counted among their students nineteen members of the Howard Division of the Vanguard of Freedom, AMAA; *American Union*, 16 November 1871.

[5] Carl R. Osthaus, *Freedmen, Philanthropy and Fraud: A History of the Freedmen's Bank* (Urbana: University of Illinois, 1976) 167, 184; Phillip D. Cory to E. P. Smith, 28 April 1869 and 13 May 1869, AMAA.

Cory was replaced by E. E. Rogers, a Yale Divinity School graduate, who as pastor of the Norwich Chapel succeeded in building a strong Sabbath school. In fact, in July 1869 he offered E. P. Smith a plan that would allow him to remain in Macon as director of religious affairs without direct educational ties to Lewis School. "I wish you would subscribe to this arrangement...to allow me to give my whole time to pastoral and missionary work with someone else...superintending ed[ucation] work."

Rogers used a variety of magazines and other published works to conduct his AMA Sabbath schools. One favorite teaching tool was the *Child's Illustrated Scripture Question Book*, published by Henry Hoyt of Boston. "We are forming more classes and putting more of our young church members into the work—and a question book will be great assistance to them," he stated. Also among the favorites were *Chapel Melodies* by Vail and Lowry, which was used in prayer meeting. *The Little Corporal Magazine*, whose motto was "Fighting against Wrong and for the Good, the True, and the Beautiful," was another early favorite, and *The Child at Home* and *The Youth's Temperance Advocate* were widely used as well. Rogers reminded AMA Field Secretary Michael E. Strieby of the importance of promoting temperance among Afro-Maconites, of "the formidable obstacles placed in the way of our workers by intemperance," and that the Macon family of teachers was "obliged to take up this department of the work and act vigorously," from year to year in both moral and religious instruction.[6]

In secular affairs, the AMA made a notable accomplishment with its Macon branch of the Freedmen's Saving and Trust Company, which had opened in October 1868. By March 1870 the total deposit on hand was $38,248, which had been collected from 500 depositors, an average deposit of $76. When the bank failed in 1874, over 700 people had deposited savings in that institution.[7]

---

[6] E. E. Rogers to M. E. Strieby, 10 March 1871; E. E. Rogers to E. P. Smith, 17 June 1869 and 6 July 1869; E. E. Rogers to E. P. Smith, 7, 15, and 29 April 1871; E. M. Barnes to E. P. Smith, 15 March 1869, AMAA.

[7] Alvord, *Ninth Semi-annual Report*, 1 January 1870, 66–67.

Lewis High School experienced considerable administrative instability during 1869–1870. In 1869, John Rockwell, who had been an able administrator and minister, resigned because of failing health. His replacement, Frederick A. Sawtelle, age twenty, a member of the Charlestown, Massachusetts, First Baptist Church, was described by his pastor, George W. Gardner, as "a young man of good abilities and unexceptionable moral and Christian character...[who] desires to go South that he may teach in a colored school." Another supporter wrote that he had "given entire satisfaction" in his school district and called him "a young man of unexceptionable character and fully qualified to fill any position to which he may be called as teacher."[8]

Apparently, Sawtelle did not find Macon to his liking, and on 28 December 1869, after only a few months as principal of Lewis School, he wrote to E. P. Smith: "Christian duty compels me to ask that I be released from my position here as early as April if it can be done without injury to the cause." Smith returned his letter urging his continuation of service until the closing of the school term. Sawtelle agreed to serve out the year, stating, "I do not question nor do I ask to be dismissed if you think the work will suffer.... I would like to make this my life work, but hope I may be fitted for wider fields of usefulness.... I do not think the work will suffer here on account of my early withdrawal."[9]

Strieby may have regretted asking Sawtelle to remain. Squabbles among the teachers soon disrupted the usually peaceful Macon "Home." Mary Hart objected to what she conceived as a romantic affair between Superintendent Sawtelle and teachers Helen Leonard and Hattie Foote. This discord eventually led to the dismissal of Foote, who asserted, "Miss Hart's object was to get Miss L[eonard] & I removed from Macon but—I have had faith to believe that the right would triumph." Nathaniel D. Sneed,

---

[8] George W. Gardner, Testimonial, 14 October 1867; Jesse Ferris or Fernd [?], Testimonial, 12 October 1867, AMAA.

[9] Frederick A. Sawtelle to E. P. Smith, 28 December 1869 and 6 January 1870, AMAA.

sometimes freedman teacher, cotton sampler, and cashier of the Macon Freedmen's Bank, addressed E. P. Smith on behalf of Foote and Leonard, saying that "they have been wrongly misrepresented and Miss Hart did try to prejudice the minds of many of my own people against them.... I beg most earnestly that they may be allowed to remain in Macon."[10]

Foote reviewed her situation with E. E. Rogers, who was of no assistance. Foote wrote, "Mr. Rogers—he knows not what to advise." Foote, angry at her dismissal, thought seriously of organizing a private school. "I can no doubt get a good one but it is suggested that this would injure Lewis High School," she said, "but really...I do not feel like being sent off." Foote saw the possible difficulty she might create in the Macon field if she branched out on her own in a private school. "Yet," she wrote, "I can live in Harmony—no doubt board can be procured for us in some colored family though we prefer remaining at the 'Home.'"[11]

Leonard also addressed Hart's charges against her and Foote. Unfortunately, Field Secretary E. P. Smith had communicated the charges to Erastus M. Cravath, "and thus," Leonard wrote, "it would be very hard to labor acceptably under him." Leonard further responded to the AMA's obvious distress at the threat of its former teachers opening a competing school. She and Foote loved Macon and the people, Leonard said, and "could not think of leaving here and a private school was our only recourse. We have no desire to work against the AMA," she said, adding, "The speaking of a private school was not meant as a threat." However, "notice has already been out that we will open a private school and it is now too late to withdraw. I deeply regret such an unpleasant ending to my connection with the AMA." A few days later the AMA asked Leonard to remain in Macon, though she was demoted to an assistant. She reported to Cravath that Foote, who was not

---

[10] Nathaniel D. Sneed to E. P. Smith, 27 September 1870, AMAA.

[11] Jacqueline Jones, *Soldiers of Light and Love: Northern Teachers and Georgia Blacks, 1865–1873* (Chapel Hill: University of North Carolina Press, 1980) 179–80; Hattie C. Foote to E. P. Smith, 26 September 1870, AMAA.

asked to stay, "left the house and will open her school on Monday if she can have the Baptist church." This break in harmony at the Macon "Home" marked the start of a trying decade for the association.[12]

Although Sawtelle's work was short-lived in Macon, he was efficient. He organized a reading room, which became the AMA's first effort to establish a library for blacks in Macon. He solicited papers and books from the association headquarters in New York. Sawtelle wrote, "I feel much interest in this as it is the first of the kind organized in the state among this people." AMA officials spoke highly of his short tenure: "In Macon the schools of the AMA, (five hundred pupils), under the care of Mr. Sawtelle, are in excellent order...the bank is starting well—a colored cashier of good ability [T. G. Steward, minister of the Macon AME Church], on deposit, $15,000." On his departure Sawtelle recommended that the association not turn control of Lewis High over to E. E. Rogers or Mary E. Hart.[13]

On 11 October 1870, a rainy Tuesday morning, the Lewis School opened its doors for the 1870–1871 school term with below-normal enrollment. The new principal was Mary E. Sands, who came to Macon from Seco, Maine. The third appointed principal in two years, Sands's commission was the first for a female in Macon. Beginning her tenure with high hopes, she wrote

---

[12] Helen Leonard to E. P. Smith, 6 October 1870; Sarah A. Stevens to E. P. Smith, 8 October 1870; Helen M. Leonard to Cravath, 25 October 1870, AMAA. Although AMA officials, seemingly with reservations, retained Leonard's services even after Hart attempted to discredit her, Leonard occupied a tenuous position in the Macon field. After apparently being demoted, she wrote to ask Cravath for direction: "At present I am an assistant in the grammar and primary schools. This unsettled state is not exactly comfortable—but is better than I deserve. I am sorry for the past. Now that my eyes are opened I see the wrong."

[13] Alvord, *Seventh Semi-annual Report*, 1 January 1869, 23; Frederick A. Sawtell to E. P. Smith, 11 January 1870 and 5 February 1870; John W. Alvord, *Letters from the South Relating to the Condition of Freedmen, Addressed to Major General O.O. Howard, Commissioner, Bureau R., F., and A. L.* (Washington, D.C.: Howard University Press, 1870) 20; Frederick A. Sawtelle, Superintendent Report April and May 1870, AMAA.

to Cravath, "It was quite rainy yesterday morning and had only seventy three scholars, today had ninety and so I suppose the number will continue to increase." A little less than two weeks later, enrollment had increased to 133 pupils. Students occupied three rooms in Lewis High, making up classes at the primary, grammar, and intermediate levels. A few months later a Miss Fitch arrived and took charge of the lower grammar department, which had forty-three pupils, relieving Sands from teaching duties. The Lewis High student population for October 1870 reached 166, for November 249 (including 58 students in night classes), and for December held at 197.[14]

Enrollments during the remainder of the 1870–1871 school term were: January 273; February 285; March 265; April 241; and May 176. Sands was able to collect $106.25 from tuition owed from December 1870. There is no question but that the growing number of independent schools, some financed by Bibb County, affected attendance at Lewis. May's drop in student enrollment also reflects the fact, however, that a number of Lewis High's best scholars were sent to teach in rural districts during late spring and summer months. (The AMA usually provided some support with books and supplies.)[15]

By 1871 Lewis High School was also competing with public schools for students. When the Freedmen's Bureau was disbanded in 1870, Georgia passed a public school law. Governor Rufus B. Bullock appointed former Georgia Freedmen's Bureau director John R. Lewis as state school commissioner. The Bibb County public school system had been organized in 1869 by a board of school commissioners acting with the court of ordinary, probably to undermine the work of the AMA; however, its public facilities

---

[14] Mary E. Sands to Cravath, 12 October 1870 and 3 November 1870, AMAA; Sarah A. Stevens to E. P. Smith, 8 October 1870, AMAA; Helen M. Leonard to Cravath, 25 October 1870; Mary E. Sands, Superintendent Reports for October, November, and December 1870.

[15] Mary E. Sands to Cravath, 4 January 1871; E. E. Rogers, 23 March 1871; Mary E. Sands, Superintendent Reports for January, February, March, April, and May 1871, AMAA.

and teachers were inadequate. Generally speaking, the nature of the public education system being created was clearly defined for both whites and blacks. In 1870 influential Georgia educator Martin V. Calvin spoke before the Georgia Teacher's Association in Savannah on the "Recent Progress of Public Education in the South." His message was that for "reasons not necessary here to enumerate, that white youth and the colored youth shall be instructed in separate schools." He further urged that "rather than submit to the great evil of social intermingling…[l]et the system be common to all, but require their schools to be separate from those of the whites in fact and locality."[16]

In May 1871, a year after the state's mandate, W. D. Williams, principal of the Georgia Academy for the Blind and Bibb County School Commissioner, wrote to E. M. Cravath about the possibility of using the association's building: "It has occurred to me that I might with great advantages to your interest cooperate with you as respect to the Lewis High School. Without going into details I think that institution with its present organization might be made the head of the system—the high school of the county for colored youth with a normal department for training teachers." Williams had visited Lewis High and "was much pleased with the teachers—the arrangements—progress of the children and what I saw generally." Nevertheless, Williams later informed AMA officials that a flaw in the state law on the nature of public support

---

[16] Henry Allen Bullock, *A History of Negro Education in the South: From 1619 to the Present* (Cambridge: Harvard University Press, 1976) 55–56; Clara Mildred Thompson, *Reconstruction in Georgia: Economic, Social, Political 1865–1872* (Savannah: Beehive Press, 1972) 335–38; Jacqueline Jones, *Soldiers of Light and Love: Northern Teachers and Georgia Blacks 1865– 1873*, 192; Martin V. Calvin, "Popular Education in Georgia: A History of Education in the State, with Suggestions as to An Approved System of Public Schools" (Augusta GA: Constitutionalist Book and Job Print, 1870) 10; Martin V. Calvin, "Recent Progress of Public Education in the South: A Paper Read before the Georgia Teachers' Association at Savannah, May 5th, 1870" (Augusta GA: Chronicle and Sentinel Steam Printing Establishment, 1870) 8; *Macon Telegraph*, 12 January 1869.

meant the state would not be able to expend funds cooperatively with the AMA, but that some of Bibb County's $10,000 education appropriation could be used to aid students unable to pay tuition at Lewis High.[17]

It was not the public schools, but the private schools, that offered the greatest competition to the AMA. Before school opened in August 1871, E. E. Rogers warned of the growing competition from denominational schools. "I think Mrs. Smith will succeed in drawing away nearly...all the scholars. Miss Foote will probably do the same thing with...scholars of the 2nd Baptist Church." The AMA resolved its problem with Foote's school by inviting her to return to the "Home," which she reluctantly accepted. "Everything seemed to indicate that I should have great success in a private school this year," Foote wrote, "and my friends were opposed to my returning to A.M.A. But for many reasons I have decided to do so."[18]

There was some question as to whether Principal Sands would return for the 1871–1872 school year. By September, Rogers had proposed to Cravath that he superintend Lewis School if Sands could not return. When Cravath declined, a disgruntled Rogers responded, "I shall cheerfully submit to your decision but it is certainly very painful to me." When school officially opened on 3 November 1871, Sands was present and wrote to Cravath that school enrollment was down due to a fair held the previous week. Moreover, Bibb County Commissioner of Schools Williams was unable to provide the promised support from county funds. Mr. Ward, the City Ordinary, did pledge five cents per day for each indigent child taught at Lewis School. Nevertheless, Sands was

---

[17] Joseph P. Reidy, *From Slavery to Agrarian Capitalism in the Cotton South: Central Georgia, 1800–1880* (Chapel Hill: University of North Carolina Press, 1992) 227; W. D. Williams to Cravath, 10 May 1871; E. E. Rogers to Cravath, 9 September 1871, AMAA; see also Susan F. Presley, "A Past to Cherish-A Future to Fulfill, Lewis High-Ballard Normal School, 1865–1900" (Master's thesis, Georgia Southern University, 1992).

[18] E. E. Rogers to E. M. Cravath, 28 August and 9, 15, 21 September 1871; Hattie C. Foote to E. M. Cravath, 27 September 1871, AMAA.

forced to turn away several students for nonpayment of tuition, and another forty-five remained delinquent. A get-tough policy was necessary in order to secure payments, Sands wrote. "Tuition must be paid the first week or...scholars will be sent away." However, in the end, because of low enrollments, she sent few students away. She undoubtedly was aware that private and county schools would eagerly embrace any available students. "I felt unwilling to send the scholars away," she said, "therefore I sustained them." Despite low enrollment and delinquent payments, Lewis High closed the term "certainly ahead of last year." Tuition fees collected amounted to $1,198, which included special funds allocated by Bibb County to aid pupils unable to meet tuition expenses.[19]

As the Bibb County Board of Education began arranging for the establishment of a common school system, as mandated by the state, local officials realized that no adequate building was available to accommodate school-age blacks in Macon. Therefore, in spring of 1872, W. D. Williams began negotiations with the AMA for the use of the Lewis School building as the primary education facility for blacks beginning that October. Although he promised to employ association teachers, Sands found Williams's plan questionable: "I am not wholly pleased with his plans," she wrote. "He does not care to work through the association…. He is obliged to contract with you for the building, but wishes to hire teachers on his own responsibility at cost of $40.00." Sands warned AMA officials of possible problems that might occur if the association lost autonomy over Lewis High School. "The colored people are very much opposed to the Southern teachers—I believe they would not be taught by them," she wrote. Eventually, the AMA and the school board reached an agreement whereby the board would

---

[19] Mary E. Sands to E. M. Cravath, 3 November and 5 December 1871; also see for 5 January and 17 May 1872, AMAA.

assume control of Lewis School and the AMA principal, Mary Sands, would be retained.[20]✗

In September 1872, County School Commissioner Williams informed AMA field agent Cravath that Miss Sands and four AMA assistants would be hired by the city board. They would be paid with state funds, and the school would open in October. The teachers were to be paid by Bibb County in scrip, which later would be made good by the state. Sands started the first term as principal under state control with eight assistants, all white. Lewis High, considered a well-organized school, taught on average just over 400 pupils per day. In addition, two schools under state auspices were taught in the African Methodist Episcopal (AME) Church. One had three black teachers and 140 pupils, while the second had sixty students and one white teacher. The Second Ward Colored Free School and the East Macon Colored Free School each had fifty pupils with one white and one black teacher, respectively.[21]

Table 2 shows the make-up of Lewis High School in October 1872.

---

[20] Mary E. Sands to E. M. Cravath, 10 June, 5 January, and 17 May 1872, AMAA.

[21] Macon City Directory, 1872, 15; W. D. Williams to E. M. Cravath, 14 September 1872; Mary E. Sands to Cravath, 16 October 1872, AMAA. Bibb County officials were accused of holding out on teachers' pay in order to gain control. Reidy, From Slavery to Agrarian Capitalism, 228.

TABLE 2[22]

Superintendent Report for Lewis High School

October 1872

Teachers	Grades	Males	Females
Sarah W. Paige	Upper Grammar	22	42
Hattie E. Foote	Lower Grammar	15	45
Louise A. Jones	Intermediate	20	39
Carrie E. Waugh	Intermediate	13	47
Sallie H. Hall	Primary	26	41
Mary E. Sands	Primary	22	29
Louise E. Nagle	Beginner	31	31
	Total	149	274
	All enrolled	423	

In January 1873, Williams left his post as Bibb County school commissioner to become president of the school board. His replacement was B. M. Zettler of Savannah. Sands was told that Williams would write to AMA headquarters in reference to the next year's plan of operation. As anticipated, under the new system January classes were large and every room was filled. The financial situation worsened under state jurisdiction, as little money was received to replace scrip that had been issued to the school by the state, and teachers' salaries were consistently in arrears. Sands requested and received $200 from AMA headquarters. She wrote Cravath, "We have been living on borrowed money," through William Barker, a city grocer, who "took the paper [scrip] given us to present to the city ordinary." The fluctuating value of scrip restricted its use in the open marketplace. In May, Sands notified Cravath, "I see no prospect of our obtaining money from the city

---

[22] M. E. Sands, Superintendent Report, October 1872.

Board of Education. I presume we will be obliged to wait until the first of July."[23]

The difference of approach between the AMA's running of the former Lewis High and the county operation may be illustrated by a controversy involving Sarah Paige, a new teacher sent by AMA to Lewis School in 1872. Unlike most of the AMA teachers, Paige, who hailed from Lowell, Massachusetts, fully endorsed the segregation principles of Zettler and the county school board members. In fact, Paige was invited along with the white Southern teachers to attend certain meetings. In a letter to Cravath, Sands reported that Zettler had said that she and the other teachers were not invited "because we entertained colored people, associated with them, and went to church with them." A number of the AMA teachers in Macon were insulted. Clearly indignant, Sands said that Zettler "could not sustain me in treating the colored people with so much respect, and the fact that we entertained them at our home was too shocking. For those reasons we could not be invited to attend the normal class that meets at his room every week." Sands added that Paige was "thoroughly southern in her principle," or she would have refused the invitation to attend meetings where other members were not invited. "She has proved herself a traitor—she is not worthy of the position she occupies. It has caused rather unpleasant feelings which is certainly a cause for regret as we have lived very pleasantly." Sands concluded, "Whatever plans you make, I hope this building will never pass into the power of southern people."[24]

The mission "Home" was further disquieted by Sarah Paige's assertion that Northern whites no longer commanded the respect

---

[23] Ida Young, Julius Gholson, Clara Nell Hargrove, *History of Macon, Georgia 1823–1949* (Macon: Lyon, Marshall and Brooks, 1950) 315; Mary E. Sands to E. M. Cravath, 3, 4 February and 13 May 1873, AMAA.

[24] Mary E. Sands to E. M. Cravath, 16 May 1873, AMAA; the consequent commissioner for state education, John Gustavus Orr, did not subscribe to using Northern teachers in black schools; see Charles T. Wright, "The Development of Education for Blacks in Georgia, 1865–1900" (Ph.D. dissertation, Boston University, 1977) 62.

of Macon's black community because of their interracial association outside the classroom. This caused Sands to report to AMA headquarters, "I have also brought a reproach upon the association for riding with a colored man on the fair ground at our May celebration. Miss Foote and I rode round the race course with Mosley, the man who has lived in our yard several years, and his wife, who has been our cook." Sands continued, "It will be exceedingly unpleasant for us to live another month as we are now living...my character is not to be questioned when I have only used every effort to win and make the people better while [Paige] only repels them." Fortunately, Paige remained at Lewis High only one year. In late May she informed headquarters that since her class enrolled only fourteen scholars, she saw no great need for her continued services in Macon. She requested Cravath to release her from all ties with the association. A few weeks later Sands wrote, "I presume Miss Paige will be in New York before this reaches you. I hope she will reach her home safely and will never venture South again."[25]

As president of the school board, W. D. Williams continued to aid in the transition of Lewis High from AMA to county supervision. On 4 June 1873, he wrote Cravath that the board wanted exclusive use of Lewis School and wished to supply it "with teachers entirely such as the Board may select." Williams set the first of October for the fall 1873 school opening and pledged to increase the teachers' monthly salary from forty to fifty dollars. The school board named the same local white teachers, except for one who had left a local white school for Lewis High when it went public and became loyal to the AMA. Williams also opposed continuation of the Mission "Home." "I do not think the home arrangement for board for your Northern ladies...[was] approved

---

[25] Mary E. Sands to E. M. Cravath, 14 May 1873; Sarah W. Paige to E. M. Cravath, 22 May 1873; Mary E. Sands to E. M. Cravath, 5 June 1873, AMAA.

by me as you will remember, last year…they can find board here in good families…more pleasantly situated."[26]

When the teachers arrived in October 1873, they continued, against Williams's wishes, to live at the "Home" and to socialize with the black community. Sands completely ignored Williams. "When I arrived I took my meals with the family in the yard and each teacher did the same until our cook arrived," wrote Sands.[27] The school year progressed without further apparent dissension. The traditional closing exercises that ended the school term consisted of "dialogues, music, and recitations in prose and poetry," according to the *Macon Telegraph*, which described the annual event. "It is due to candor to state that the young Africans' ideas seem to have been cultivated with great diligence, and give promise of vigorous growth." Children show respect for "a strong hand by principal, Miss Sands." The article continued, "Indeed, it required but a glance, to see the Amazonian characteristics of the lady, which is a fortunate circumstance, as she unites good judgment and fair amount of discretion with her muscular gifts."[28]

The *Telegraph* also paid tribute to the four white Southern teachers at Lewis School, Mrs. Baber, Miss Reese, Mrs. Nagle, and Miss Hall, "who are now doing excellent service in that capacity." Superintendent Zettler, said the article, addressed the crowd with a few remarks of "practical advice and counsel to parents and children…. He is the right man in the right place." In a separate paragraph the *Telegraph* lamented of the Northern teachers, "Still we are forced to recollect that they are nothing more or less than missionaries regularly accredited from the parent concern who mercifully vouchsafe to redeem and regenerate the benighted South." This statement reflected the white Maconites' biggest concern regarding the AMA: teaching social equality, if not in class,

---

[26] Mary E. Sands to E. M. Cravath, 5 May 1873; W. D. Williams to E. M. Cravath, 4 June, 8 August, and 9 September 1873, AMAA.

[27] Mary E. Sands to E. M. Cravath, 18 October 1873, AMAA.

[28] Mary E. Sands to E. M. Cravath, 6 January 1874, AMAA; *Macon Telegraph*, 28 June 1874.

by example. Said the *Telegraph*, "They visit the negroes, eat with them, and, practically illustrate and inaugurate social equality." Whites claimed that the AMA was doing blacks a disservice, and their mission was "an errand of mischief," which could only harm and retard black progress.[29]

The AMA's religious program was failing to win widespread support from the black community. Reverend E. E. Rogers, discouraged over his inability to attract black members to the Congregational Church, resigned to pursue an evangelical career in the far west. Rogers suggested that he be replaced by a black minister, as "there is a prejudice on the part of this community against a white face which only those on the ground can feel." Congregationalism, with its Northern white ministers clearly did not appeal to the Afro Maconites. Nevertheless, the New York office chose to send Rev. Frank Haley, the popular former minister, who was white.[30]

In April 1873, to the delight of Mary Sands and the AMA teachers, Haley and his wife returned to Macon. Haley had successfully served during 1867–1868 as the first pastor of Norwich Chapel, but when he commenced work for the second time in Macon, he found the situation a "vast discouragement." The congregation, he felt, needed discipline. Most of his former members had left the church, and those who remained, "from twelve to thirty-five," he found "cold and inactive." Haley complained that Norwich Chapel was "literally beset with prejudice and opposition. Every colored church in the city is in open or secret hostility to this." The African Methodist Episcopal Church had erected a large brick edifice costing $50,000 nearby. "The church with its extensive galleries is literally thronged sometimes to overflowing twice every Sabbath," he noted, and the AME Church,

---

[29] *Macon Telegraph*, 28 June 1874.

[30] E. E. Rogers to E. M. Cravath, 4 September and 4 April 1872; E. E. Rogers to E. M. Cravath, 10 January 1873, AMAA; Joe M. Richardson, *Christian Reconstruction: The American Missionary Association and Southern Blacks, 1861–1890* (Athens: University of Georgia Press, 1986) 149.

under the lead of T. G. Stewart, had "assumed an openly and aggressively hostile attitude toward the Congregational Church."[31]

Some black church members were urging the appointment of an African-American minister for Norwich Chapel. Willis Epps, a well-known church figure, had been approached on the subject on several occasions before Haley arrived. Epps and some of the other members rejected the suggestion on the grounds that "it would be an unmanly yielding to an unreasonable prejudice." However, later, even Epps thought it "best to have a colored pastor" because many blacks were "kept away by the simple fact that a white man is its pastor." Haley wrote Cravath, "The brethren feel that this church never can be built up unless we get a colored minister." The word on the streets in Macon was, "Oh, that is just no church at all." Haley saw developing a "strong prejudice against suffering white ministers to be pastors of colored churches. I think no means are neglected to increase this prejudice. It is certainly extensive and growing."[32]

Haley did note, however, that many African Americans who were members of other churches sent their children to the AMA Sabbath schools. He contended that these parents were purely selfish, sending their children to the chapel school because they think they will receive better instruction there. By August 1874, Haley had concluded a black minister was necessary if the Congregational Church was ever to be successful. "It is best to give this church the trial of a colored pastor," he said, since "the prejudice against a white man as pastor of any colored church in Macon is very strong—and very widely disseminated. It is also increasing." Thus the association appointed William A. L. Campbell, a Jamaican-born black minister, to replace Haley.[33]

---

[31] Mary E. Sands to E. M. Cravath, 4, 6 April 1874; Frank Haley to E. M. Cravath, 15 June 1874, AMAA; *American Missionary* 18 (November 1874): 247–48.

[32] Frank Haley to E. M. Cravath, 15 June 1874, AMAA.

[33] Frank Haley to E. M. Cravath, 15 June, 28 August 1874, AMAA.

Campbell was an 1874 graduate of Howard University's theology department. The AMA had commissioned him to teach in North Carolina in 1873 while he was a second-year seminarian. Upon his arrival in Macon in September 1874, Campbell made a favorable impression on Haley: "He seems to be a very intelligent gentlemanly man. He is well instructed in the word of God." Campbell was less impressed with the church. He found it "to be made up of young people [Lewis High Students], it having very few heads of families attached to it, perhaps not more than a dozen if that." The Sunday school had a fair attendance, but not as "might be expected in a city like this." In general "I am satisfied," Campbell wrote, that "we will be successful here in time. We can't expect too much as Congregationalism is new among the people and it is not to be wondered at even if it has done so much for them that they do not take hold of it any faster."[34]

The church parsonage was not made available to Rev. Campbell and his family because, according to the AMA, it was in disrepair. Campbell asked the AMA to provide him a parsonage, saying that if not fitted with one, "they will say all over the city so long as a white man was here they let him have the parsonage but as soon as they get a colored man they let him shift for himself." Willis Epps wrote to Cravath that local blacks already were suspicious of the AMA and that since Campbell was not provided with a parsonage, conditions were likely to worsen. "The colored people have said already that you would not employ a colored minister, and now to take the parsonage away will injure your work

---

[34] Frederick D. Wilkinson, *Directory of Graduates Howard University 1870–1963* (Washington, D.C.: Howard University Press, 1965) 62; Maxine Deloris Jones, " 'A Glorious Work': The American Missionary Association and Black North Carolinians, 1863–1880" (Ph.D. dissertation, Florida State University, 1982) 93; Richardson, *Christian Reconstruction*, 199; Frank Haley to E. M. Cravath, 26 September 1874; W. A. L. Campbell to E. M. Cravath, 1 October 1874, AMAA.

in Macon. I hope you will consider the matter well. This is the way it appears to me."[35]

Campbell was dissatisfied on other counts as well. "I must tell you frankly," he stated, "that except my salary be raised, should I receive an offer from a church...I will be forced to accept it." Campbell further indicated that fifty dollars a month might be good salary for a teacher, but "that sum is totally inadequate for a minister and his family in a civilized community." Again in October, Campbell complained of his salary, which he compared to that of the previous ministers who had made $1,000 a year and were provided with a parsonage. Campbell said he "felt that my color had something to do with it." When Cravath responded with a lecture on the need to sacrifice for the cause, Campbell replied, "I was inclined to think that the old, but false idea of asking men of African extraction or origin to do work of the same nature and under the same circumstances...for a smaller salary, still existed in your mind and from which I was determined to disengage myself." Campbell added that he too had forgone his family and friends "to aid in lifting up a degraded and oppressed branch of the human family for whom Christ died." AMA officials did restore the parsonage to Campbell, but did little to raise his salary.[36]

At the same time, the AMA also was embroiled in ongoing negotiations with Bibb County over Lewis High. Superintendent Zettler had proposed in 1874 to abandon further use of the school as a public building under the prevailing arrangement, which required the board to employ some AMA teachers; he wanted to replace them with Southern teachers. Zettler also argued that Lewis School provided little room for recreational activities for children when school was not in session or during recess. Haley urged Cravath "not to sell or lease one dollar's worth of this property—nor make any further concessions to Bibb County School Board." When the public school board learned that blacks

---

[35] Frank Haley to E. M. Cravath, 26 September 1874; Willis Epps to E. M. Cravath, 27 September 1874, AMAA.

[36] W. A. L. Campbell to E. M. Cravath, 14, 20, 27 October 1874.

were moving to assume support of Lewis School, it at last agreed to employ three AMA teachers and to open six rooms in the building. Joseph Clisby, Williams's replacement as president of the Bibb County School Board, informed Cravath that board members would appoint Sands principal for another year at seventy dollars per month and two additional teachers at fifty dollars per month.[37]

Lewis School opened in the fall of 1875 under the same conditions as the previous year. Four hundred students were enrolled in classes taught by five teachers. However, at the end of the school year, Superintendent Zettler recommended that the city cut all ties with Lewis High and conduct classes in different building throughout the city during the summer months. White schools were to go on as usual, from fall through late spring, but schools for blacks would run from July to the beginning of winter only. This plan was clearly intended to make black youth available for agricultural and other work and to rid the city of Northern missionary teachers. Local blacks quickly held a public meeting to discuss the implications of Zettler's proposal and passed a resolution concerning the educational welfare of their children. "The Board of Education has now changed the period for schools to the very hottest months of summer, commencing with the 5 July and teaching through the warmest months of the year." Campbell reported to Cravath that many parents decided to send their children to the Roman Catholic schools, two of which had opened in 1874 in Macon and made no distinction regarding race, rather than be "tyrannized."[38]

A "Board of Responsible Managers," composed of twelve local citizens, was appointed to cooperate with the AMA in behalf of Afro Maconites to assist in making Lewis High self-supporting. They drafted and sent a petition to George Whipple and M. E.

---

[37] Frank Haley to E. M. Cravath, 15 June, 11 August, 9 September 1874; Joseph Clisby to E. M. Cravath, 19 September 1874, AMAA.

[38] Mary E. Sands to E. M. Cravath, 27 October 1874, AMAA; B. M. Zettler to E. M. Cravath, 3 June 1875; W. A. L. Campbell to E. M. Cravath 10 May, 30 June, 1 July 1875, AMAA.

Strieby at AMA headquarters in New York, which stated, "The point on which this attack concentrates itself is this fact: these missionaries from the North recognize and heartily concede to us our rights...and for this offense, against the prejudices of the white citizens of Georgia, these missionaries are...ostracized from all southern homes and society." It was signed by Jefferson Long, former U. S. congressman from Georgia; Willis Epps, a leading member of Norwich Chapel; Edwin Belcher, Postmaster; Edwin Woodliff, a Macon entrepreneur; L. A Rutherford, M.D. and sometimes minister; and others who made up the city's black artisan and professional class. The petition further stated that if the Macon Board of Education took control of Lewis High so as to exclude Northern teachers, blacks would refuse to patronize the schools and "if necessary again open our churches and send North for what teachers we may need in addition to those we may ourselves be able to furnish."[39]

On the evening of 7 July 1875, Lewis School was set on fire. The beams and flooring between the schoolhouse and chapel were well saturated with coal oil, and a black man seen loitering about the area had been under the chapel. The fire was discovered by Mrs. Campbell in time to be arrested, and black and white citizens alike promptly came to extinguish the flames. Central City Light Infantry, under Captain DeLion, contributed to the effort, and the city provided guards through the night. Fortunately, Lewis School suffered only minor damage to the flooring and a few other areas.[40]

The local board of education voted, in keeping with Zettler's recommendations, to discontinue providing support for Lewis High under the prevailing arrangement. Campbell urged the AMA to "appoint one or more competent colored teachers on the same terms that you employ white teachers." He went on to say, "My

---

[39] Petition to AMA headquarters from Macon leading black citizenry; W. A. L. Campbell to E. M. Cravath, 2 July 1875, AMAA; James Nathaniel Eaton, "The Life of Erastus Milo Cravath: A Guiding Light in an Era of Darkness" (Master's thesis, Fisk University, 1959) 75–76.

[40] W. A. L. Campbell to Cravath, 8, 12 July 1875, AMAA.

wife has been a teacher of high standing in the public schools of Washington, D.C." A graduate of the normal and preparatory department of Howard University, Mrs. Campbell (a Catholic) had eight years of experience. She had been elected principal of Lincoln School on Capitol Hill, but came South after marriage. The AMA never gave her a commission. That she was Catholic and that the association had some difficulties with her husband may have been factors. The AMA was more responsive to William Scarborough, a graduate of Lewis High, Atlanta University, and Oberlin College, who requested an appointment at Lewis High or somewhere in the South.[41]

Scarborough and Campbell represented a growing movement toward black participation in their own institutions. The AMA usually accommodated the demands when "qualified" individuals were found "as the people seem to wish to have part colored teachers, and it will please them to know the ass[ociation] will employ them." Shortly after the AMA commissioned Scarborough, who took charge of the intermediate rooms, trouble broke out. Macon teacher Annette Lynch reported to Strieby: "I hear from Deacon Epps and Mr. Campbell that there is among some of the people a feeling of dissatisfaction in regard to the AMA work here." Apparently a growing number of individuals wished Scarborough to have the highest room and an increase in salary. "If they have no confidence in the AMA or its teachers, perhaps it will be best to withdraw us from here," Lynch stated. She was afraid that Scarborough would set up an opposition church school in his hometown.[42]

By 1876, Campbell's ability to gain a large congregation was in doubt, and his influence among his peers in the AMA was in question. Church attendance was still smaller than that for the

---

[41] W. A. L. Campbell to Cravath, 28 July, 11 August 1875; William Scarborough to Cravath, 18 September 1875, AMAA.

[42] William Scarborough to E. M. Cravath, 18 September 1875; Annetta Lynch to M. E. Strieby, 25, 26 October 1875; Annette Lynch to D. E. Emerson, 15 November 1875, AMAA.

Sabbath school, and the condition of affairs soon became chaotic. "It seems impossible for the church to hold together under the present pastor," wrote teacher Sarah Bierce. According to Bierce, Campbell's "passionate and hasty speech angered some leading members and they did not attend at all." She contended that not more than fifteen members were present at any one meeting. She also noted the "influence exerted by his wife who rules him completely" and "his threats to go over to the Catholics." Bierce wrote to Delia E. Emerson at headquarters, "I will say here what I think would be best for the church and school, that we have another pastor and a white one and married." The relationship between the Campbells and local teachers and church members continued to deteriorate. Wrote Bierce, Mrs. Campbell "has not spoken to the teachers for some time and greeted us iceberg fashion."[43]

Finally in May 1876 leading members from Norwich Chapel petitioned AMA headquarters for Campbell's removal: "We the undersigned members of Norwich Chapel, after much deliberation, petition the immediate removal of Rev. W. A. L. Campbell...his manners and acts repel rather than win the people, especially the young...the Catholic influence exerted by his wife causes much feeling in the church and cripples what power he may have for usefulness." Campbell defended himself saying that a few members, namely, Edward Woodliff, Willis Epps, William Jones, and John Brooks "have been the moving agent in this matter." He also claimed that the AMA had "become dissatisfied with me because I did not use my influence to have the school go on next year on a similar basis." Secretary Strieby asked for Campbell's resignation.[44]

Campbell replied to the petition and letter from Strieby:

---

[43] Sarah C. Bierce to D. E. Emerson, 13 March, 19 April 1876, AMAA. In 1883 Delia Emerson was asked to create a Bureau of Women's Work to inform women's groups about the AMA and support its activities. See Fred L. Brownlee, *New Day Ascending* (Boston: Pilgrim Press, 1946) 280.

[44] Petition from Norwich Chapel to M. E. Strieby, May 1876; W. A. L. Campbell to M. E. Strieby, 27 May 1876, AMAA.

I do not think you are acting very wisely...in asking my immediate resignation when you know how hard it has been for other ministers in this field...it is a very unfortunate thing for this church that it has got into the habit of changing pastors so frequently.... I am sorry to say that I have got the ill will of one or two people of my congregation on account of using my influence in getting the Lewis High School for the colored public schools. This I did because I sense that it was for the greatest good...of the masses and not for a few selfish men that want to carry things their way.

In mid-July L. A. Rutherford replaced Campbell until a permanent minister could be selected.[45]

Macon's establishment of separate free elementary schools for blacks had caused enrollment at Lewis School to drop for the 1875–1876 school term. Secretary Strieby made a special trip to Macon in March 1876 to tend to matters regarding the Macon Board of Education and Lewis High. In April 1876 Lewis High had only eighty-two pupils enrolled, and of these, approximately one dozen "who never studied grammar or geography" were admitted to normal training, creating a problem for those in the higher branches with proper training. Nevertheless, Sarah Bierce informed headquarters that "a promising class from the grammar room will be ready to enter the first year of the normal course next October."[46]

At the Bibb County Board of Public Education's annual session in June, a delegation of Afro Maconites conveyed their displeasure over the changing of the school year. They also exerted

---

[45] W. A. L. Campbell to M. E. Strieby, 27 May 1876; L. A. Rutherford to M. E. Strieby, 1 August 1876, AMAA.

[46] W. A. L. Campbell to E. M. Cravath, 3 September 1875; S. C. Bierce to M. E. Strieby, 19 April 1876; S. C. Bierce to D. E. Emerson, 6 May 1876; M. E. Strieby to G. Whipple, 24 March 1876, AMAA.

pressure on the board about schools without seats and the use of planks for benches in various buildings throughout Macon. After a lengthy discussion, the board agreed to meet their demands. The board resolved "to discontinue the existing summer school of colored pupils...and to reestablish the school at the Lewis High building on the first of October." The arrangement gave total control to the local board. Superintendent Zettler expressed gratitude for the AMA's offer to place Lewis High "at our disposal on such liberal terms," and he assured Strieby in writing that "so far as my part of the contract is concerned, all its requirements shall be carried out in the utmost good faith."[47]

With such controversies settled, the fall term of 1876 at Lewis High School began on a high note. However, on Wednesday evening, 13 December, around 10 p.m., fire again broke out, and this time the school, along with Norwich Chapel, was totally destroyed. The *Telegraph* reported that the fire was accidental, and that although the engines were slow to come, the firemen worked exhaustively in an effort to abate the flames. Lewis School reopened in the basement of the John A. Rockwell home while plans were made to rebuild using the insurance money. The makeshift school was without a principal, as Mary Sands had resigned to take a position as receptionist at Atlanta University. The fire was the culmination of the many problems that the AMA endured during the 1870s. But the association, in weathering the storm, had set the stage for first-rate education for African Americans in Macon.[48]

---

[47] "Public Education," *Macon Telegraph*, n.d., ca. June 1876, AMAA; "Echoes From the South," *Christian Recorder*, 2 June 1876; B. M. Zettler to M. E. Strieby, 12 June 1876.

[48] Webster to D. E. Emerson, 18 December 1876, AMAA; *American Missionary* 21 (February 1877); *31st Annual Report of the AMA*, 1877, 74.

CHAPTER 4

FROM LEWIS HIGH TO
BALLARD NORMAL SCHOOL
1877–1893

Lewis High School had ended the turbulent Reconstruction era (1865–1877) by going up in flames. Having lost a school in what it considered a prime location in Macon, the AMA used the $5,000 fire insurance money to rebuild. AMA teachers and personnel, headed in the interim between principals by the Congregational pastor, entered the 1878 new year with prayers. Lewis High reopened on 24 March 1878. The new school, although much smaller than the one it replaced, served a dual purpose as school and church. Designed by Professor T. N. Chase of Atlanta University, the school was a two-story brick building with gas lighting; three rooms made up the lower floor, and the upper floor served also as the Congregational Church. Although one large room could seat 110 pupils, a smaller room for recitation could fit approximately twenty-five to thirty comfortably. The new high school enrolled only ninety-three students. The normal program continued to help provide black teachers for Central Georgia, particularly after Georgia instituted its common school system for both whites and blacks.[1]

---

[1] *Macon Telegraph and Messenger*, 14 December 1876; *Georgia Weekly Telegraph*, 27 March 1877; *American Missionary* 21 (August 1877): 1–2; *32nd Annual Report of the AMA*, 1878, 69.

Beginning in the 1880s, the AMA accepted that it had lost its fight with white Georgians on the notion of social equality for blacks; to continue its customary course as it had during Reconstruction was a lost cause. From this point on, the association made a direct attempt to gain support for its educational programs and turned a deaf ear to politics, especially when divorced from educational overtures. The history of efforts to destroy Lewis High School by fire (the first one failed, but the second succeeded) indeed was convincing enough for the AMA to pursue a different course with white Southerners.[2]

Breaking the gender barrier for the second time, in 1879 the AMA brought in Christine H. Gilbert to serve Lewis School as principal. Only eighty-eight students were enrolled upon her arrival. Perhaps few students could afford the tuition payments: The association charged one dollar per month for upper grades and seventy-five cents for primary students. Gilbert, a long-time resident of Fredonia, New York, came to Macon as an experienced teacher, having served eight successful years at Minnesota State Normal School. Other new arrivals included the Congregational minister Rev. Stanley E. Lathrop and his wife Sarah, a teacher from New London, Wisconsin, and teachers Belle Haskins, Delmore, Kansas, and C. M. Babcock, Newburyport, Massachusetts.[3]

Beginning in the late seventies, AMA officials, whenever possible, involved leading white Maconites—and white Georgians generally for that matter—in their educational affairs. Greater community involvement in the school's closing exercises was aimed at improving public relations with both the black and white communities. The AMA followed the concept for these exercises as it had been set forth in 1868:

---

[2] Joe M. Richardson, *Christian Reconstruction: The American Missionary Association and Southern Blacks, 1861–1890* (Athens: University of Georgia Press, 1986) 257; Edmund L. Drago, *Black Politicians and Reconstruction in Georgia: A Splendid Failure* (Baton Rouge: Louisiana State University Press, 1982) 163.

[3] *33rd Annual Report of the AMA*, 1879, 45; *34th Annual Report of the AMA*, 1880, 43; *Macon Telegraph*, 30 May 1880.

Examinations, and also exhibitions, if properly conducted, should be held at the close of every term. School boards and patrons must require such examination, and teachers are to prepare for it and invite attendance. The aim of these exercises is not a sensational display, covering over general defects, or a "showing off" of the few best pupils; but a true exhibit of the condition of the whole school. When this is done a healthy stimulant is diffused throughout the entire term, felt by both pupil and teacher. Parents in considerable numbers, though neglecting their children at other times, are often seen at such examinations.

Our schools for freedmen specially need them. They give opportunity to all for criticism, and to patrons to learn for themselves the facts. Persons indifferent to the schools are drawn in. Enemies even are disarmed when they become eye witnesses of what is accomplished.... It should also be said, that without this important event, the schools, as the end of the year approaches, deteriorate, and usually terminate with a loss of both interest and attendance.[4]

In keeping with this tradition, on 28 May 1880, Lewis High held its closing exercises as 110 students assembled for examinations. The *Macon Telegraph* remarked that "a more intelligent and well behaved body of colored youths cannot be found anywhere." Special guests for the occasion included local ministers Rev. George McDonald and Rev. Joseph Key. According to the *Telegraph*, both "expressed themselves highly gratified with all that they saw and heard, and when called upon responded with neat

---

[4] John W. Alvord, Inspector's Report of Schools and Finances, U.S. Bureau of Refugees, Freedmen and Abandoned Lands (Washington, D.C.: U.S. Government Printing Office, 1866–1870); see *Sixth Semi-annual Report*, 1 July 1868, 75.

and appropriate address." The association no longer solicited remarks from Afro-Maconites such as Jefferson Long and Henry McNeal Turner. It had become more accommodating to local whites. The *Telegraph* editor encouraged local citizens to give continued support to Lewis High for the good work it accorded the "colored people of Macon."[5]

The 1880–1881 school year started off with 109 students enrolled. Lewis High continued to enjoy favorable relations with local white citizens by avoiding politics. Leading white citizens, including long-time supporter W. D. William, principal of Georgia Academy for the Blind, Professor Link, and Rev. J. W. Burke of Burke publishers, as well as blacks—particularly those whose children were students—remained loyal to the AMA. During 1881 closing exercises, students demonstrated lessons from classes in reading, arithmetic, philosophy, and geography. As usual, the *Telegraph* commented favorably and mentioned the quality of the teachers—all of "fine education and well calculated to succeed in their vocation." Later, the scholars marched in to the school anthem, "Be Faithful, Firm, and True," followed by music, a reading of Psalm 23, and the Lord's Prayer. On a lighter note, songs included "From Grave to Gay" and "The Farmer's Boy," which was delivered by the boys in a whistling chorus with "great gusto and a good deal of musical harmony." The editor concluded, "Lewis High School is one of the best schools in our city, and its thoroughness, discipline and marked excellence should win for its teachers the hearty approval and support of all classes of people. All teachers are ladies of high attainments and successful teaching.... All these AMA schools are doing good work in the South."[6]

Lewis opened in fall of 1881 with more staff changes. W. A. Hodge of West Rosendale, Wisconsin, had assumed the principalship. Hodge, a graduate of Ripon College, accompanied by his wife, came to Macon highly recommended. She was one of "four lady helpers who would take high stand in our best Northern

---

[5] *Macon Telegraph*, 28 May 1880.

[6] *Macon Telegraph*, 1 June 1881; *Macon Telegraph*, 2 June 1881.

schools." The other new staff members were Alice M. Lindsley of Avondale, Illinois, Jennie M. Woodworth, Clyde, Ohio, and Carrie M. Park, West Boxford, Massachusetts. The Lathrops stayed on to continue their service to the church. The *Macon Telegraph* published a complimentary article, in which it encouraged a large fall enrollment: "The assistant teachers are all highly educated and capable ladies. We hope for a full attendance of scholars."[7]

When school commenced, however, only sixty-four students were present, although attendance was expected to increase within a few weeks. Many of the poorest pupils picked cotton in the fall to help with family expenses and to raise their tuition. Enrollment usually increased in December, after crops were harvested. Average attendance for the three months was for October sixty, November seventy-four, and December eighty-four. The lowest grade was composed of beginning students in reading. The majority of the students were taking the teachers' training program in the normal department. The remaining students took classes in advanced arithmetic, elementary algebra, physiology, physics, and higher level geography and Latin.[8]

Normal school training had become a primary concern for those interested in black education. Throughout Georgia, the success of an adequate common school system depended on a steady supply of competent black teachers. In his *Fourth Annual Report*, the state school commissioner of Georgia expressed grave concern over the problem of finding teachers to staff its rapidly growing school system:

> The want of suitable teachers for our colored schools is a much more serious matter. The number of colored men or women capable of teaching, is very small—so small as to interfere seriously in many places

---

[7] *Macon Telegraph*, 2 October 1881; *American Missionary* 37 (August 1883): 234–36.

[8] W. A. Hodge to AMA, n.d., ca. 1882, AMAA; *American Missionary* 35 (November 1881): 336.

with the chance of establishing colored schools. To employ the rude and untutored, is evidently a waste of money, and yet it has often been found necessary to relax the requirements for obtaining a teachers' license very much, in order to procure a teacher at all.[9]

The need for black teachers to meet this growing demand in Macon and Central Georgia propelled officials at Lewis High to increase normal student enrollment and accelerate the output—sometimes at the expense of satisfactory training. For example, in 1878 there were only fifteen students enrolled in normal training at Lewis School, but each year thereafter the normal student population increased dramatically: to fifty-three in 1879, fifty-nine in 1880, and ninety-six in 1881.[10]

At the same time, students in some of the other school programs were facing obstacles to their advancement. When W. A. Hodge assumed charge of Lewis High, he undertook to restructure its grading system. Although Lewis High had been graded in 1868 under John A. Rockwell, Hodge wrote to AMA headquarters that such "a course of study seems to have been adopted but not sustained." As he restructured various grades, some members of the senior classes of 1881 and 1882 were retained without being given certificates or diplomas. As a result, in protest, some students left school to secure employment.[11]

Hodge pleaded with AMA officials for a larger, adequate schoolhouse to accommodate more students in four complete grades, each with its own teacher. This seems an "imperative need," he wrote. Even though Lewis School had rebuilt after the fire, its

---

[9] *Fourth Annual Report of State School Commissioner Submitted to the General Assembly of the State of Georgia, at Its Session in January, 1875* (Savannah: J. H. Estill, Public Printer, 1875) 24; hereafter cited *Fourth Annual Report of State Commissioner.*

[10] *32nd Annual Report of the AMA,* 1878, 69; *33rd Annual Report of the AMA,* 1879, 45; *34th Annual Report of the AMA,* 1880, 43; *35th Annual Report of the AMA,* 1881, 54.

[11] W. A. Hodge to AMA, n.d., ca. 1882, AMAA.

facilities were inadequate for the present needs, and classrooms were crowded, especially during recitation in the normal training program.[12]

As there were no other schools in Central Georgia for black students beyond sixth grade, it was not unusual for students to come to Macon from as far as thirty to fifty miles away to attend Lewis High. One family with four children moved to Macon from coastal Georgia, near Brunswick, so that the children could be educated above the elementary level. Hodge was convinced that if Lewis had a good, low-cost boarding department, it could render better services toward meeting black Georgians' aspirations for an education.[13]

The AMA cooperated with state and city officials to develop plans to train teachers and leaders. If Macon and Central Georgia were to have competent teachers, particularly elementary school teachers, Lewis High would supply this need. The state encouraged teachers to acquire a reasonable knowledge of gardening, household arts, and simple woodwork in addition to methods of teaching, school management, and educational psychology. Education officials urged administrators at private institutions such as Lewis School to seek the advice of public authorities in order to become a vital part of the school system.[14]

In fact, Lewis High was one of only a few secondary schools in existence for African-American youth in Georgia. The lack of training facilities resulted in a majority of Georgia's black teachers being poorly prepared. During this period, fewer than one in five black school teachers in Georgia had more than a grammar school education. More able individuals sometimes sought other professions, but, due to segregation, opportunities for Georgia's

---

[12] Ibid.

[13] Ibid.

[14] Thomas Jesse Jones, ed., *U.S. Department of the Interior, Bureau of Education, Negro Education: A Study of the Private and Higher Schools for Colored People in the United States*, Bulletin No. 39, vol. 1 (Washington, D.C.: Government Printing Office, 1916) 78–79; *Fourth Annual Report of State Commissioner*, 1875, 24.

black population were limited to only a few occupations outside of teaching. To add insult to injury, pay for teachers was miserable, and, in general, women were paid less than men, and blacks less than whites. Further, the prevailing attitude, as stated in the state superintendent's report, was that "our colored teachers everywhere throughout the state, can live for much less than the white. When [N]egroes enter any other field of labor requiring skill and intelligence, their services can be procured for much less than you have to pay white men."[15]

Not only were Lewis High graduates and advanced students who went out to teach poorly paid, but most also had to endure the wretched conditions found in ill-equipped, one-room schools. Unable to obtain decent buildings, many rural teachers taught in shanties in the county and on the outskirts of small Southern towns in Central Georgia, where they encountered extreme conditions. Quite a number of "student teachers" left Lewis in the early spring, when weather conditions were not as cold, and continued for nearly three or four months into the summer. In many of these rural areas, these few months offered the only opportunity for black youths to attend school. One Lewis High graduate described the conditions of his rural teaching assignment in a letter to association headquarters in New York: "I have worked faithfully for three months. I was assigned to a place where there was no schoolhouse or church. The people had their meetings under an arbor. I worked with the patrons of the place until they built me a school-house.... My school numbers thirty-nine scholars. I have received several petitions from the colored people asking me to come again and teach for them."[16]

---

[15] Jones, *Negro Education Public and Private,* 71; *Fourth Annual Report,* 24; Donald L. Grant, *The Way It Was in the South: The Black Experience in Georgia,* ed. Jonathan Grant (Secaucus NJ: Carrol Publishing Group, 1993) 234; *Report of the State School Commissioner of Georgia,* 1883–1884, 1884, 31.

[16] *American Missionary* 36 (August 1882): 239; *34th Annual Report of the AMA,* 1880, 58.

While the need for more able black teachers was echoed throughout the South, beginning in 1882 a far greater cry was being heard on the subject of industrial education. The first industrial schools for blacks in Macon were begun by skilled black artisans who taught in poorly equipped public schools financed by Macon during Reconstruction. Most black artisans in Macon were brick masons, carpenters, tailors, blacksmiths, plasterers, and painters, and Afro-Maconites could be found working on the "finest buildings," catering to a white patronage. Industrial education was radically strengthened in 1882 by the efforts of one man. Northern textile manufacturer John F. Slater, a supporter of the Congregational Church, donated one million dollars for the "uplifting of the lately emancipated population of Southern States, and their posterity, by conferring on them the blessing of Christian education." The Slater Fund was used primarily to aid private and denominational institutions devoted to teacher training along industrial lines.[17]

The Slater Fund Board had set as its guidelines: "That so far as practicable the scholars receiving the benefit of this foundation shall be trained in some manual occupation, simultaneously with their mental and moral instruction." As a rule, Slater support aided schools in any of several areas: general appropriations, support for normal instructors, or supplemental salaries, sometimes paying the salary of an industrial instructor, sometimes providing suitable tools for a school's industrial department. Slater trustees espoused a philosophy that sought out industrial education as a means of

---

[17] J.W. Brooks and T.C. Dempsey, Teacher Monthly Reports, May 1869 and March 1870, Bureau of Refugees, Freedmen and Abandoned Lands, Educational Division, Georgia; *Proceedings of the Trustees of the John F. Slater Fund for the Education of Freedmen* (Baltimore: John Murphy & Company, 1883), 21; hereafter cited *Proceedings of John F. Slater Fund*; Dorothy Orr, *A History of Education in Georgia* (Chapel Hill: University of North Carolina Press, 1950) 308; John E. Fisher, *The John F. Slater Fund: A Nineteenth Century Affirmative Action for Negro Education* (New York: University Press of America, Inc., 1986) 2–4, 13; Benjamin Brawley, "Early Effort for Industrial Education," The Trustees of the John F. Slater Fund, *Occasional Papers*, No. 22 (1923) 2–5.

making a more "self-reliant and self-supporting population," especially those individuals who were to become teachers. Supporters of black education argued whether industrial or literary-industrial education fitted pupils for leadership in their community, as symbolized by the head, hand, and heart.[18]

The AMA had introduced industrial education in some of its earliest schools in the 1860s. However, in order to obtain Slater Foundation money, new industrial shops were opened or expanded in many association schools. The AMA made clear that industrial education was not intended to replace the regular curriculum in its schools. "And we urge all school authorities to use industrial training, not in order to make the Negro a mere toiler, but to evoke a nobler manhood and womanhood by the discipline of intelligent labor." AMA officials further stated that industrial education, in its view, "did not accord with the modern southern theory of Negro education that it should be distinct from other education...of those poor people destined to be a permanent peasant class, and no more." Nonetheless, the AMA gladly accepted $200 in 1882 from the Slater Foundation to procure an industrial arts instructor.[19]

In 1883, a two-room wooden annex was added to Lewis School. The upper story was used as a library and the lower served as a carpenter shop. In that year the Slater Fund again gave $200 to Lewis School, and the following year Slater funding more than doubled to $500. This increase in funding from the Slater Foundation was enough to prompt the association to change the name of Lewis High to Lewis Normal Institute, reflecting both its industrial and teacher training components. The Slater Funds were

---

[18] Jones, *Negro Education Public and Private*, 81, 257; *Proceedings of John F. Slater Fund*, 1883, 14, 15, 20.

[19] *Proceedings of John F. Slater Fund*, 1883, 15; Isabel C. Barrons, ed., *First Mohonk Conference of the Negro Question held at Lake Mohonk, Ulster County, New York, June, 5, 6, 1890* (Boston: George H. Ellis, Printer, 1890) 19, 130–31; Augustus F. Beard, *Crusade of Brotherhood: A History of the American Missionary Association* (New York: Kraus Reprint Co., 1970) 163.

used to pay the salary for an instructor in carpentry. In 1886, the foundation appropriation again was $500.[20]

The *American Missionary* reported that male students generally exhibited "eagerness and enthusiasm" for industrial work. The shop teacher, Mr. Burger, instructed the boys in wood-working tools for an hour and a half each day after school. Many students were so enthusiastic that sessions were frequently extended to three or four hours. Local businesses and Northern Sunday schools donated supplies and money to improve the shoproom or to purchase more tools, lumber, and other materials. AMA officials limited industrial work, for financial reasons, to wood-working, mostly carpentry, and mainly the use and care of tools and general construction and repairs on furniture and school facilities. Several students participated in a sort of work-study program, which paid their board and tuition; others were able to earn half of their board by working for the association and paying the remainder with money earned during summers from skills they learned in industrial shop.[21]

By 1885, industrial education had become an essential element of Lewis Normal Institute. Eighty girls were being instructed in various branches of sewing, which had been introduced in 1881 by Elizabeth Lathrop, wife of the Congregational pastor. In carpentry, twenty-one boys were learning wood turning, plain furniture making, painting, and varnishing. New principal Livia A. Shaw, from Oswego, New York, reported that boys from Lewis Normal Institute were "earning a good living by work at the carpenter's trade...[and] one of the graduates made benches for the rooms in which he taught." Atticus G. Haygood, first agent of the Slater Fund, gave good ratings to Lewis Institute's industrial work. Haygood, a minister, former president of Emory University and an

---

[20] *Proceedings of John F. Slater Fund* (Baltimore: William K. Boyle & Son, 1888) 23; *36th Annual Report of the AMA*, 1882, 37.

[21] *American Missionary* 38 (November 1884): 340; *American Missionary* 39 (February 1885): 51; *American Missionary* 46 (April 1892): 130; *Proceedings of John F. Slater Fund*, 1888, 44.

advocate for black education and advancement, had been instrumental in Slater's decision to establish the fund. Haygood made occasional visits to Lewis throughout his tenure.[22]

In January 1888, Haygood reported to the trustees of the Slater Fund that "I have just returned from Macon, Georgia. Our Lewis Institute there is now under splendid management and the industrial idea runs through everything." After a return trip to Macon a few months later, he reported being "greatly pleased with its present management under Livia A. Shaw." He noted noticeable improvements at Lewis in all departments with regard to thorough teaching and an efficient industrial training program. While in Macon, Haygood delivered a Sunday sermon at the Congregational Church.[23]

In the late 1870s, while the AMA was overseeing the evolution of Lewis School, its church in Macon also was undergoing changes. On 12 December 1878, the Georgia Conference of Congregational Churches was formed in Macon, representing churches in Tennessee, Mississippi, Alabama, and northern Georgia. In all, twelve churches made up the newly organized conference, which replaced the Central South Conference and the defunct Southeast Conference. Three of the churches were represented by white ministers, while the remaining nine were pastored by black ministers who had received their training in AMA schools. The Congregational Church associated with Lewis was never particularly popular in Macon. The Georgia Conference met in Macon in 1881, hoping to increase the membership of the local church. Members visited Lewis High to talk to students and teachers and listen "to the songs of the children," and a few

[22] *Proceedings of John F. Slater Fund*, 1883, 14; *Proceedings of John F. Slater Fund*, 1888, 23–24; Louis D. Rubin, Jr., ed., *Teach the Freedman: The Correspondence of Rutherford B. Hayes and the Slater Fund for Negro Education*, vol. 1 (Baton Rouge: Louisiana State University Press, 1959) 175, 231. Haygood's numerous publications include *Our Brother in Black: His Freedom and His Future* (1881) and *Pleas for Progress* (1889).

[23] *American Missionary* 42 (March 1888): 63; Rubin, *Teach the Freeman*, vol. 2, 6, 110–11; *Proceedings of John F. Slater Fund*, 1888, 23.

ministers gave "short spicy addresses." On Sunday, the conference supplied several "colored" churches with guest preachers, among whom was AMA Field Secretary Rev. J. E. Roy. Unfortunately, the Macon visits yielded only twelve new members for the local Congregational church. Still, officials ended their conference with the statement, "Congregationalism in the South is not a failure."[24]

While Congregationalism never took hold in Macon as the AMA officials had hoped, the AMA was successful in brightening the educational outlook for blacks in that city, especially after a gift from AMA supporter Stephen Ballard. Ballard, a wealthy philanthropist, born in Andover, Massachusetts, moved to New York, where he attained success in the leather and belting business. He organized the White, Potter & Paige Company and served as its treasurer. Ballard had donated money to AMA schools in Tougaloo, Mississippi, Salisbury, North Carolina, Berea, Kentucky, and Macon. After visiting Lewis Normal Institute in 1888, he decided that its physical plant needed to be improved. Ballard's plans and specifications for a new school building met the approval of AMA executive officers. In all he appropriated $12,000 to construct a new brick school building large enough to house 600 students. Ballard's sister donated another $7,500 for a girls dormitory, to be named Andover Hall, after their hometown. At the same time, AMA officials voted to enlarge the mission "Home."[25]

On 14 February 1889, a large group of people, including AMA officials, state officials, and leading black and white Maconites, gathered for the dedication of the new AMA school. The *American Missionary* remarked upon the mixture of races: "They were seated

---

[24] *American Missionary* 33 (February 1889): 50–51; *34th Annual Report of the AMA*, 1880, 65; *Macon Telegraph*, 10 and 13 December 1881. Other ministers who spoke were Rev. Floyd Snelson, who was a missionary in Africa and was affiliated with Dorchester in Liberty County, Georgia, and Rev. E. Kent of Atlanta.

[25] AMA Executive Committee Minutes, 11 June 1888, 446, American Missionary Association Archives, Addendum; obituary of Stephen F. Ballard, *New York Times*, 13 August 1901; Rubin, *Teach the Freedman*, vol. 2, 27.

upon the platform together with the colored ministers of the town, and in the most innocent manner it so happened that there would be a white minister and a colored sitting next to each other the whole length of the platform." Since the Lewis School building had been destroyed in 1876, a number of whites had publicly supported the school. From the superintendent down, there seemed to be a real desire on the part of those present to see the new school succeed. The opening exercises were delivered by Bibb County School Superintendent B. M. Zettler. Additional remarks were made by Dr. Greene, a leading black physician, and three local ministers, Dr. Warren of the First Baptist Church, Dr. Jennings of First Presbyterian, and Rev. Miller of the Washington Avenue Presbyterian Church. Dr. Augustus F. Beard, Corresponding Secretary of the AMA, made the final address.[26]

All of the speakers at the dedication commented on black progress and on the continued importance of education as an elevating tool for blacks. Zettler "expressed his interest in all educational matters in Bibb County and confirmed his good will gratitude...to help on a good cause." Dr. Warren, who recalled having been present at the Lewis High dedication back in 1868, observed that the AMA's efforts in Macon had resulted in growth and character-building and advised the crowd to support "these Yankees" whose skill and energy helped provide for Macon's black population.[27]

Dr. Jennings' remarks centered around "the needs of a high aim and firm purpose in accomplishing any important work in life." Dr. Greene, instead of addressing "the common attempt to solve the Negro problems by stirring up discontent among people and making them dissatisfied with present conditions," thanked the AMA for its work in Macon. AMA Secretary Beard stated that the association's aim for blacks in Macon was "to supplement the efforts of those who are trying to help themselves, that true independent manhood and womanhood shall be developed."

---

[26] *American Missionary* 43 (April 1889): 101.
[27] Ibid.

Beard then announced that "with the hearty concurrence of General Lewis that...this school should hence forth be known as Ballard Normal School." After a vote of thanks to Stephen A. Ballard, everyone visited the new eight-room, brick facility that had just been dedicated. "The beauty and convenience of the rooms, the fine pictures on the walls, the beautiful desks and chairs for the teachers, the elegant Steinway piano, the bell and the handsome stoves, were all noted and heartily commended." Unfortunately, Stephen Ballard was unable to attend the dedication and to share a delightful moment for supporters of the school.[28]

Ballard's generous gift had so enlarged the school's potential for educational development that Haygood, after careful review of various other institutions, in 1889 increased Slater funding for Ballard to $800. Ballard continued to emphasize teaching the use of hand tools, but did not follow the Hampton or Tuskegee models or the educational principles espoused by Booker T. Washington and Samuel Armstrong, which advanced an almost exclusive industrial school curriculum at the expense of an academic course of study. However, Ballard did take advantage of the situation by promoting industrial education at its closing exercises during this period. Students displayed the tables, boxes, bookshelves, towel racks, lap-boards, screens, and even an easel and pulpit they had made. Girls were taught needlework based on the theory of household economy. Ballard also made a conscious effort to teach good health and methods of caring for those unable to take care of themselves due to disease or accident. The contents of the school library, which had grown to over 1,600 volumes, probably the largest in the city, reflected this growing tendency toward better health among blacks in American cities.[29]

---

[28] *American Missionary* 43 (April 1889): 102; When Stephen A. Ballard died in 1901, he donated his estate, estimated at $150,000, along with stocks from White, Potter, and Paige Manufacturing Company, to the AMA. See *New York Times,* 23 August 1901.

[29] *Teach the Freedman,* vol. 2, 57–60; James D. Anderson, *The Education of Blacks in the South 1860–1935* (Chapel Hill: University of North Carolina Press, 1988) 66–67; Donald Spivey, *Schooling for the New Slavery: Black Industrial*

With improved facilities and a growing enrollment, Ballard Normal emerged in the 1890s as a premier educational institution for African-American teacher training in Georgia and the South. Although students sometimes found it difficult to pay the meager amount needed for tuition and board, a small emerging black middle class continued to send their children to Ballard. Families who could not afford AMA tuition had to settle for an elementary education for their children at public expense. Despite competition from public schools, enrollment at Ballard was averaging more than 500 pupils per year, having reached its highest point since the creation of a public school system. One reason for Ballard's success was the industrial training introduced and fostered by the Slater Foundation, which created "more friends among Southern white men than all [the] speeches and writing put together." Taking advantage of this favorable racial climate Ballard continued to

Education, 1868–1915 (Westport CT: Greenwood Press, 1978) 54; *American Missionary* 44 (June 1890): 184; *American Missionary* 45 (August 1891): 298–99; *American Missionary* 46 (August 1892): 267–68; Atlanta University Publications, No. 1, *Mortality Among Negroes in Cities,* ed. Thomas N. Chase (Atlanta: Atlanta University Press, 1903) 23; Atlanta University Publications, No. 2, *Social and Physical Condition of Negroes in Cities* (Atlanta: Atlanta University Press, 1897) 17.

provide even greater numbers of professionals for Macon and became the primary provider of teachers for Central Georgia.[30]

[30] *44th Annual Report of the AMA*, 1890, 32; *45th Annual Report of the AMA*, 1891, 57–58; Atlanta University Publications, No. 7, *The Negro Artisan: A Social Study*, ed. W.E.B. Du Bois (Atlanta: University of Atlanta Press, 1902) 41.

CHAPTER 5

THE ADMINISTRATION OF
GEORGE C. BURRAGE
1894–1909

In the fall of 1894, AMA Secretary Augustus F. Beard appointed George C. Burrage of Worcester, Massachusetts, to succeed Francis T. Waters as principal of Ballard Normal School. Ballard's enrollment was 568, making it one of the largest of all the association's secondary schools, second only to LeMoyne in Memphis, Tennessee. During the next fifteen years, Principal Burrage made a number of improvements aimed at raising the caliber of the school. He standardized the general curriculum, strengthened the academic programs, and continued to emphasize normal and industrial education. He also attempted to develop alumni support and to help subsidize programs and bring about physical improvements for the benefit of the students.[1]

One way in which Burrage and other Ballard officers attempted to stimulate support from alumni and the community was through an expansion of the traditional closing exercises at the end of each school year. The first event designed to entertain and impress parents and friends of students was the "Junior

---

[1] *Straight Ahead, Annual Report of the American Missionary Association,* New York, 1933–1934; *Catalogue of Ballard Normal School* (Macon: J.W. Burke, 1908).

Exhibition," held about a month before the end of school. Pupils in all grades performed exercises consisting of dialogues, recitations, and music, both vocal and instrumental. Next, a week before the term ended, members of the graduating class and their guests were received at the teachers' "Home." The purpose of the reception was to encourage a final discourse among students and teachers. On the last Sunday of the school year, the graduating seniors assembled for an annual sermon by the local Congregational minister. On the following Wednesday, Visitors' Day, parents and friends observed the various grades' industrial department exhibitions and viewed selected written assignments from other subjects taught at Ballard. At noon, the domestic science class served lunch to illustrate what they had learned in cooking. The following day, the commencement exercises took place, complete with essays and recitations by students and a speech by an invited guest.[2]

The end-of-year activities that marked the close of Burrage's first school year in office were begun on 26 May 1895. As usual, to impress visitors, special steps were taken in preparation for the occasion. That particular year new carpet was installed (a gift from the women of the First Congregational Church of Evanston, Illinois) and decorations of white clover and ivy were added to spruce up the facilities. The Rev. J. R. McLean, pastor of the Macon Congregational church, preached the sermon, titled "Unconscious Influence," in which he reminded students that the best examples were offered by righteous living. Music "was not wanting for the occasion," and after the daylong written examinations that tested the year's work, an evening concert by the Ballard choir was held to entertain parents and friends.[3]

Members of each class, from kindergartners to seniors, made presentations to show their progress. That year, the fourth graders' examination consisted of reciting the fifth and a part of the sixth chapter of the book of Matthew, while the fifth graders named and spelled all the books of the Bible. Exhibits of industrial work

---

[2] *American Missionary* 49 (August 1895): 261.
[3] Ibid.

attracted the most attention, featuring, from the domestic science classes, samples of "patching, matching, piecing, buttonholes" and a variety of well-made garments. The class in woodwork displayed "window frame sashes, stepladders, little boxes with pretty covers of inlaid wood, and many other useful ornamental articles." The domestic science class prepared a "table spread with dainty eatables" to be sampled by all those present.[4]

The activities concluded with the commencement exercises in the Congregational Church. A large, standing-room-only audience, made up of the "best colored people in Macon," was present. Five young women read essays and a young man gave an oration. The Rev. Henry Hugh Proctor, a Fiskite and 1894 graduate of Yale University Divinity School and pastor of the First Congregational Church of Atlanta, gave the commencement address. He spoke about the characteristics of true manhood and urged his black listeners not to become cross and distressed about present conditions, but to be confident and move on. "Do not be afraid of being called an upstart," Proctor advised. And he continued, "An upstart is one who has started up, and the upstarts of one generation will be the aristocrats of the next." He commended those "martyrs of the washtubs and the cooking stoves" for their efforts to ensure their offspring the advantages of schooling that had been denied them. After Proctor's address, Principal Burrage presented the diplomas and made some closing remarks to the effect that the graduates' education had just begun.[5]

The following year's closing exercises followed the pattern of activities just described. One special highlight of the 1896 ceremonies was the choir's rendition of the Jubilee Songs, a medley of "Steal Away," "Get on Board," and "Swing Low," under the direction of former Fisk Jubilee Singer, Lincolnia C. Hayes, an 1888 Ballard graduate who, after earning a B.A. from Fisk in 1892, had

---

[4] Ibid., 261–62.
[5] *American Missionary* 49 (August 1895): 262; Rayford W. Logan and Michael R. Winston, *Dictionary of American Negro Biography* (New York: W. W. Norton, 1982) 505–06.

returned to Macon to teach at her alma mater. The annual address was delivered by Rev. S. A. Peeler of the M.E. church, who "did not enumerate the things the Negro can do," but clearly articulated in laymen's terms what *anyone* must do in order to obtain success.[6]

In 1898, Rev. Dr. Haynes from the AMA church in Athens, Georgia, delivered the commencement address. The next day, at a final assembly for nongraduating students, a "promotion list" was read with new grade assignments for the next year, and the school term ended.[7]

When Burrage assumed the management of Ballard, the school's primary objective continued to be normal education, to prepare "Christian teachers to meet the increasing demands of the public schools both in rural communities and in towns." Ballard still was the only high school in Macon for blacks. Although the Slater money had been used to incorporate industrial training into the high school program at Ballard and other AMA schools, industrial education was never allowed to replace either the traditional liberal and classical curriculum intended to ground students in pedagogic methods or the college-preparatory courses that provided the necessary instruction to individuals seeking higher education.[8]

The graded system at Ballard in 1901 began with a "lowest primary" kindergarten room, with fifty to seventy students who exhibited "every indication of intelligence." Burrage contended there was "little difference between them and children of the same age in the white schools in respect to their ability to learn." The

---

[6] *American Missionary* 50 (April 1896): 280–81; *50th Annual Report of the AMA*, 1896, 45; J. B. T. Marsh, *The Story of the Jubilee Singers Including Their Songs* (London: Hodder and Stoughton, 1897) 109–10. Hayes later resigned from Ballard to go on tour throughout the North and East as a Jubilee Singer, raising money for the AMA. She also taught at a high school in Galveston, Texas; see *Catalogue of Ballard Normal School*, 23.

[7] *American Missionary* 52 (November 1898): 127–28.

[8] *55th Annual Report of the AMA*, 1901; *American Missionary* 55 (January 1901): 58; James D. Anderson, *The Education of Blacks in the South, 1865–1935* (Chapel Hill: University North Carolina Press, 1988) 66–67.

next grade, second primary, instructed by Martha Williams Logan (Ballard 1888), was moved to the church basement after enrollment increased from eighty-seven to 150 students. Next were the third and fourth primary. The fifth grade received quite a number of its students from the country schools, as the public schools in many rural districts in Georgia provided no instruction at this level. During this period the state accepted no obligation to educate blacks beyond five, six, or (at best), eight years.[9]

Grammar (junior high) school pupils were taught arithmetic, geography, and language "with fair success." The grammar department was divided into two grades, and because the city of Macon assumed responsibility for only six years of education for black youths, Ballard Normal provided space for two seventh and two eighth grades. These two classes were not always filled, for by the time they reached this level, many parents assumed that their children were old enough to work and could no longer be afforded the luxury of an education as they were needed to help with family expenses. Other youths felt they had approached the "limit of their intellectual capacity" or no longer showed the interest for further schooling.[10]

The largest schoolroom at Ballard contained the five classes or grades that comprised the normal department, or high school. In 1901 these classes were taught by two teachers and the principal, who held class in his office. A recitation room adjoined the office. Students in normal classes studied algebra, geometry, American and British history, and literature.[11]

Ballard's full term program was unusual for Central Georgia, and badly needed. Outside of Macon, in the rural agricultural districts, schools typically were opened in November or December, after cotton crops were harvested, and kept open for only three

---

[9] *American Missionary* 55 (January 1901): 58–61; *Catalogue of Ballard Normal School*, 23; *American Missionary* 56 (July 1902): 329–28.

[10] H. Paul Douglass, *Christian Reconstruction in the South* (Boston: Pilgrim Press, 1909) 223–24.

[11] *American Missionary* 55 (January 1901): 61–62.

months. In many of these outlying areas, the three months constituted the entire school term, although some districts added a term of two months in late spring after the cotton was planted and "chopped," or hoed. As was mentioned earlier, Ballard students from the fifth grade up taught many of these schools in rural counties, in most cases providing the only instruction available. A number of Ballardites depended upon the teaching to earn money for the next school year. Many taught in "benighted communities," doing pioneer work in "cabins or in churches with no school furniture." The conditions in these remote districts mirrored the circumstances of the earliest freedmen schools, having few books and buildings that could "scarcely be kept warm in winter," although few complained or became discouraged.[12]

By comparison, Ballard was a modern, well-equipped facility. Since 1888, the Ballard physical plant had consisted of a brick school building on New Street, a workshop for teaching industrial arts, and a two-story brick Congregational church. Across the street from the school building stood the teachers' "Home" and Andover Hall, the girls' dormitory. The "Home" was "a quaint old southern house" for teachers that also accommodated a few boarding students. The kitchen and dining room of the "Home" also were used to teach practical cooking in domestic science classes. Soon after 1900, classroom space, which included the main school building, the first floor of the church, and a small building previously used as a workshop, had reached capacity. As a result, discussions began about abandoning the first three grades to accommodate increased enrollment in the higher grades.[13]

As enrollment in the higher grades grew, so did the number of graduates, from seven in 1900 to twenty-eight in 1907. Ballard's class of 1909 consisted of twenty-one graduates, eighteen girls and three boys. The school's stated purpose was primarily to prepare students to teach and for higher education, and the 1909 class demonstrated that its purposes were being achieved. Sixteen of the

---

[12] Ibid., 58–61.
[13] Ibid., 62.

female graduates took teaching positions, and two of the young men went on to college. Although some of the Ballardites who became teachers pursued advanced study, most, like the sixteen members of the class of 1909, were hired after obtaining the normal certificate. While schools in urban areas (including Ballard) sought the more experienced or college-educated teachers (by 1901 the teaching staff at Ballard had come to include some black teachers from both the North and South), these normal-trained "beginners" usually started their teaching careers in isolated rural areas of Georgia and were able gradually to " 'work in' with experience toward the city."[14]

During Burrage's tenure as principal, Ballard's program offerings became better defined. The standard normal curriculum equipped students to become teachers, while the college-preparatory courses readied students for higher education. Middle school students were required to take some courses in industrial education. By the end of Burrage's tenure, Ballard was concentrating on the intermediate, or grammar, and secondary levels of education. The institution's goal was to "offer the colored people of central Georgia the best possible opportunities for obtaining a standard high-school education with special normal and industrial training."[15]

By 1901, increased enrollments in the upper classes led the AMA to drop the first two grades at Ballard. Even so, Ballard enrollment increased, from 519 in 1900 (with the lower grades) up to 585 in 1907. The AMA was progressively able to abandon the lower grades because state and local authorities increasingly had made arrangements to provide elementary education to local black children. Many black Maconites, however, resisted the dropping of the lower grades at Ballard, pleading for "the continuance of primary instruction on the ground that otherwise their children will get poor teaching in unsanitary buildings, often on immoral

---

[14] Elise Campbell, *Ballard Normal School* (New York: American Missionary Association, 1909) 2–3; reprinted in *American Missionary* 63 (October 1909).

[15] *Catalogue of Ballard Normal School,*1908, 6.

streets." Despite parent concerns, Burrage found it necessary to drop the first two grades at Ballard to provide more space for upper-level instruction.[16]

When school opened for the 1905–1906 school year, Ballard Normal's enrollment was 460 students, 105 of whom were enrolled in grades ten through twelve. These high school students were taught by a staff of three teachers and Principal Burrage. Another eighty-two boys took lessons in manual training. That year, Andover Hall, the girls' dormitory, housed fifty-two girls, and eight male boarders were accommodated locally; however, sixty potential students were turned down for want of housing.[17]

Reflecting the AMA's emphasis on academic subjects and moral teachings, the primary curriculum for the third- and fourth-year students consisted of literature, writing, spelling, oral and written arithmetic, geography, and the Bible. However, after gifts from the Slater Fund beginning in 1882 brought increased emphasis to industrial training, industrial education was introduced into the Ballard curriculum. The AMA considered the ages from twelve to fifteen the time when youngsters should be taught industrial education, so during the fifth year industrial education was introduced, and sewing (for girls) and shop work (for boys) remained part of the curriculum through the ninth grade.[18]

During the Burrage years, Charles E. Middleton, a graduate of Atlanta University, taught shop. All male students from the fifth to the ninth grade received instruction in manual training from Middleton, whom Burrage described as a taskmaster, "thoroughly equipped for his work," who set high expectations and ably brought his students to reach those expectations. The industrial curriculum for the fifth grade consisted of knife work, drills in the use of the gauge, measurements, tri square, and cutting surfaces

---

[16] Douglass, *Christian Reconstruction in the South*, 224; *American Missionary* 63 (October 1909): 655.

[17] *American Missionary* 59 (January 1905): 8.

[18] *Catalogue of Ballard Normal School*, 11, 15–16.

from thin wood. The next year, simple wood cuts were done, and the seventh grade students studied the use of woodworking tools. In the eighth grade, special instruction was given in the use of the circular saw, jigsaw, hand lathe, and blueprints. The best of the student work, which included carpentry and chair caning (some of which they could take home), was highlighted at the end-of-year exhibitions. During the final year of manual training, pupils were introduced to mechanical drawing, geometric figures, orthographic and scale drawing, oblique projections, working drawings, and architectural drawing.[19]

The AMA insisted that industrial education include female as well as male students. Girls in grades five to nine were required to take sewing, and Ballard hired a special teacher to give domestic science lessons modeled after those in Northern schools. Students learned the practical side of darning and mending and became familiar with cutting fabric and making patterns for new garments. Girls in grade five learned basting, stitching, hemming, and putting on bands. The sixth- and seventh-grade students were exposed to lacing, placketing, buttonholes, sewing on buttons, and making undergarments and shirtwaists. By the ninth grade, the students were making dresses and other items. They were required to supply the necessary materials if they wished to keep the finished product.[20]

In addition to sewing, the older girls took classes in cooking. The kitchen at the teachers' "Home" and later a remodeled room in Andover Hall were used for this training. During the first half of the school year, classes covered the fundamentals of cooking and preparing meals. For the second term, class members took turns planning and preparing their own meals under a teacher's supervision. Students did their own marketing and other chores

---

[19] *American Missionary* 61 (August 1907): 174–75; *Catalogue of Ballard Normal School 1911–1912* (Macon: Anderson Printing Co., 1911) 6; *Catalogue of Ballard Normal School*, 16.

[20] *American Missionary* 61 (August 1907): 175; *Catalogue of Ballard Normal School*, 7, 15.

connected with the essentials of homemaking. On occasion, the domestic science students invited friends and teachers to take meals with them, and, of course, they prepared and served food for the end-of-term exhibitions.[21]

Although the industrial education programs were strong, the AMA never considered industrial education more than a sidelight at Ballard. The school's primary mission was to train teachers and to prepare black students for higher studies. Because of its liberal and classical bent, secondary students preparing for college took Latin, Greek, algebra, geometry, physics, history, geography, literature, and Bible classes on the life of Christ and poetical books of the Bible. As the high school division of Ballard continued to grow, so did the number of teachers. The school's 1908 list of high school instructors included George C. Burrage, Danvers, Massachusetts, Ph.B., principal and teacher of Greek and physics; Elise Campbell, Millburn, New Jersey, B.A., history, English, English literature, and senior reviews; Raymond G. Von Tobel, Waterbury, Connecticut, Ph.B., mathematics, botany, and American history; Katharine Maynard, Brockport, New York, Latin, physical geography, and science; and Carolyn P. Johnson, South Boston, Massachusetts, B.A., physiology, algebra, arithmetic, and ethics.[22]

In keeping with the strong religious atmosphere established at Ballard, AMA officials required the observance of strict codes of social and classroom conduct. The rules were few, but they were "enforced with firmness and impartiality." Boarding students could not "receive calls on the sabbath," and permission was required from the principal or preceptress for those wishing to leave the school premises. Students were expected to adhere to appropriate applications of the Golden Rule: "Do unto others as you would that they should do unto you." In this regard, students were required to show "respect for the rights of others in all things" by maintaining

---

[21] *American Missionary* 61 (August 1907): 174–76; *Catalogue of Ballard Normal School*, 7.

[22] *Catalogue Ballard Normal School*, 3, 9.

"neatness and cleanliness" and showing "courtesy towards teacher and pupils." Any pupils found guilty of damaging school buildings or furniture incurred the expense of repairs. School officials tolerated neither "profanity nor the use of tobacco" on the Ballard campus. Everyone who entered Ballard was "regarded as giving a promise to abide by its rules and regulations, and when anyone becomes careless or wilfully disobedient, he is liable to suspension or expulsion." To the AMA, discipline was parental and aimed to "develop Christian manhood and womanhood."[23]

Throughout Ballard's history, financial problems were acute. This was especially true during Burrage's tenure, a time in which the association was forced to abandon many of its schools and concentrate on a few select secondary schools and colleges. As one of the largest secondary schools under AMA auspices, Ballard was fortunate to be among those that survived. The association had to increase the school's funding somewhat over a period of time because tuition and students' fees were far from sufficient to meet the operational expenses of the institution. For example, during Burrage's fifteen-year tenure, from 1894 to 1909, the amount of student tuition fees collected amounted to $44,395, while total operating expenses for the school for that period came to approximately $88,566, about twice the amount raised by student fees. Of the total amount, nearly half went toward teachers' salaries, with another portion used to support the minister of the Congregational Church, and the remainder going toward furnishings and general repairs.[24]

By supplementing the money raised by student fees for board and tuition, the AMA made it possible for "students of small means to secure an education." Students who lived on campus paid eight dollars per month for board and tuition and were required to work one hour per day. Others who could not meet the eight dollars were able to do additional hours of work to defray their expenses.

---

[23] Ibid., 7, 8.

[24] *49th to 63rd Annual Report of the AMA*, 1895–1909, 72, 61, 71, 68, 78, 88, 87, 79, 79, 61, 66, 67, 63, 70, 67, respectively.

The charge for tuition alone was one dollar per month for students in grades three to eight, $1.50 for those in ninth grade, and $1.25 for those in grades ten to twelve. Pupils who desired to take instrumental music lessons were charged twenty-five cents per week plus an additional fee of fifty cents per month for the use of the piano and organ for one period a day. Textbooks were available for rent at five cents per month for scholars in grades three and up. All school bills were due on the first of the month and were payable one month in advance.[25]

At the turn of the century, Burrage was forced to make some needed changes in Ballard's physical plant. On several occasions, improvements were made on direct order from the AMA headquarters in New York. The association voted in November 1900 to appropriate one hundred dollars to paint a building at Ballard, but then transferred $300 from a fund earmarked for scheduled improvements to the Ballard teachers' "Home" to aid a sister institution Dorchester in McIntosh, Georgia. Over the next few years, however, many improvements were made on the buildings and grounds through the aid of $2,670 from the AMA's Daniel Hand Fund, including the construction of fire escapes for school buildings and street improvements. In 1909 the AMA executive committee approved allocations not to exceed $1,500 from sale of property in Macon owned by the AMA to make improvements on the teachers' "Home." Of this amount, one hundred dollars was used to install a bath and toilet.[26]

---

[25] *Catalogue of Ballard Normal School*, 7, 8.

[26] AMA Administrative Committees Minutes, 13 November 1900, AMAA; Daniel Hand was a Connecticut philanthropist who in 1888 contributed one million dollars to the AMA to create the Daniel Hand Educational Fund for Colored People. The interest was to be used to support various projects, such as improvements for AMA school facilities. For more on Hand, see Joe Martin Richardson, *Christian Reconstruction: The American Missionary Association and Southern Blacks, 1861–1890* (Athens: University of Georgia Press, 1986) 105; and Augustus Field Beard, *A Crusade of Brotherhood: A History of the American Missionary Association* (New York: Kraus Reprints Co., 1970) 256–57; AMA

Despite the continuing shortage of funds, Ballard Normal School saw tremendous growth during Burrage's administration. Rapid increases in higher-grade enrollment underscored the need for additional space, larger classrooms, and adequate dormitory facilities to accommodate the growing number of older students. Ballard had to turn away nearly half of its potential out-of-town pupils for lack of dormitory space. The school needed an assembly and study room, a music room, and larger accommodations for the sewing department and domestic science as well as a lunchroom for day students.[27]

Burrage constantly solicited funds from friends and alumni to help improve facilities and defray costs for students. According to the 1908 *Catalogue of Ballard Normal School*, Burrage launched a campaign to raise $4,000 and to encourage donations of table linens, sewing materials and furnishings for domestic science classes, books and periodicals for the library, and reference books for students in the higher grades.[28]

By the time Principal George Burrage resigned in 1909, to seek a cooler climate, Ballard had achieved its mission of becoming primarily a college-preparatory and normal secondary school. During his fifteen years of dedicated service, he had directed Ballard toward gaining a national reputation as an institution of excellence for African Americans in middle Georgia.[29]

Administrative Committees Minutes, 10 November 1903, 13 December 1904, 11 December 1906, 11 May 1909, 9 November 1909, 8 November 1910, AMAA.

[27] *Catalogue of Ballard Normal School*, 109–10.

[28] *Catalogue of Ballard Normal School*, 9.

[29] *Catalogue of Ballard Normal School*, 9–10.

CHAPTER 6[1]

BALLARD UNDER
RAYMOND G. VON TOBEL
1911–1935

Ballard's most devoted leader during the first third of the century was Raymond von Tobel. He was appointed principal in 1911 and would serve in that capacity until his death in 1935.

When AMA secretary H. Paul Douglass appointed him principal in 1911, von Tobel was a young teacher at the school, with only three years' experience. He had been teaching mathematics, botany, and American history in the high school department at Ballard since 1908. Von Tobel had served only two years as principal when, in 1913, the AMA sent him to Fort Yates, North Dakota, the government headquarters of Standing Rock Reservation for Sioux Indians, to head a small mission school. The following year, due to the poor health of his wife, Flora, von Tobel was transferred back to Macon and resumed the principalship at Ballard, replacing acting principal Christian F. Klebsattel. During his long and peaceful tenure at the school, von Tobel helped lay the groundwork for the modern school that Ballard eventually became.[2]

---

[1] This chapter appeared in slightly altered form in *The Georgia Historical Quarterly* 82 (Summer 1998).

[2] *Missionary Herald* 131 (September 1935): 430.

Von Tobel was born 15 June 1884 in Terryville, Connecticut, the son of William and Harriet Goodwin von Tobel. He earned the bachelor of philosophy degree from Brown University in 1907, after which he went to Ballard as a teacher. While principal, he attended a summer session at Harvard University in 1926, and after 1931 took the courses in administration and supervision at the University of Georgia School of Education that were required for state-accredited high school principals.[3]

According to AMA Secretary Fred Brownlee, von Tobel represented the "New England missionary at best." An effective administrator, von Tobel was able to keep the school afloat despite economic hard times and changing administrators. Equally important, he managed to maintain peaceful relations between the black and white communities in Macon. During his tenure, in fact, top AMA officials, who were inclined to visit troubled schools most often, rarely visited Ballard. A confidential AMA report praised von Tobel's administrative skills and described him as "very lovable; gets on with everyone." He was a patient man who loved children and the outdoors.[4]

Under von Tobel's administration, a well-qualified faculty, black and white, provided elementary, secondary, and normal training at Ballard. Secondary teachers at the school usually had degrees from Northern and Western colleges, while those who taught at the lower levels, until the 1930s, were generally Ballard graduates with normal certificates. The faculty at Ballard did more than just direct the intellectual development of its students. In keeping with tradition, school policy during von Tobel's administration placed supreme emphasis upon cultivating moral

---

[3] *Missionary Herald* 131 (September 1935): 430; Raymond J. Pitts, "Tribute is paid to Prof. [von] Tobel," n.d., ca. 1935; "The Accredited High Schools of Georgia," *Bulletin of the University of Georgia* 35 (September 1934): 8–9; von Tobel papers, Amistad Research Center, Tulane University, New Orleans, Louisiana; hereafter cited as von Tobel Papers.

[4] Ibid.

and spiritual values, considered the main ingredient for sound Christian character.[5]

Von Tobel began his tenure at Ballard at an auspicious moment in the school's history. Outdated facilities were about to be replaced with new, modern ones. In 1911 the AMA sold a dormitory lot to the city of Macon for expansion of the city hospital and used the proceeds to acquire adjoining property. In 1914 the AMA sold that property, along with all property that comprised Ballard's physical plant, to the city hospital for $36,000, with the provision that it could retain use of the school property until June 1916, with an option to rent the Congregational church building for an additional six months. The AMA then acquired the Schofield property, five acres approximately two miles west of the old site, for nearly $8,000. At that time, the AMA executive committee voted to erect a new school building and to spend an additional $4,500 for a new teacher's home, to be equipped with gas and electricity. Classes would continue in the old building until the new school could be completed. Twenty-five thousand dollars was set aside to build a new church. Construction began soon after.[6]

Although many changes were underway at Ballard during the 1913–1914 school year, when von Tobel was absent, the school flourished under acting principal Klebsattel. Enrollment reached nearly 400, with more than 150 in the upper grades. The majority of Ballard students were locals, but in 1913–1914 some thirty came from other areas of Georgia. A few rural students were able to pay the cost of boarding, including one young man who walked from Georgia's backwoods with a few clothes and a savings of eighty-

---

[5] *Catalogue of Ballard Normal School,* 1911–1912, 8–9; *Ballard Normal School Bulletin,* n.d., ca. 1930, von Tobel Papers.

[6] *Catalogue of Ballard Normal School,* 1911–1912, 8–9; *65th Annual Report of the AMA,* 1911, 45–46; hereafter cited as AMA Annual Reports; Executive Minutes Book, 1913–1919, AMA, 9 March 1915, 82; 9 November 1915, 141; 14 September 1915, 124; 14 March 1916, 158; 11 January 1916, 150; 8 February 1916, 154; American Missionary Association Archives, Tulane University; hereafter cited as AMAA.

seven dollars to attend the school. Many nearby students who could not afford to board walked as many as six miles every day. Two sisters walked over ten miles daily over bad roads, even in inclement weather.[7]

During 1913–1914, Ballard had a faculty of fourteen, including seven blacks and seven whites, three males and eleven females. Six of the teachers taught secondary classes. Classes were generally well organized, and textbooks were current. Elementary pupils were admitted beginning at the fourth grade, and seventh and eighth grade students were required to take industrial course work. At the secondary level, courses were arranged so that students could elect the Latin, or college preparatory, course or could do industrial work for the first two years and teacher training in the last two years. Of the fifty-eight students in the eleventh and twelfth grades during the 1913–1914 school year, eighteen took the college preparatory course and forty teacher training. All students were required to take core courses: four years of English, three years of mathematics and history, and one year of science.[8]

Ballard was run efficiently on limited funds. The report for 1913–1914 shows that student tuition amounted to $4,124, which was matched by $3,952 from the New York office plus $416 from donations specifically stipulated for Ballard. Of the $8,492 budget, $4,148 went for teachers salaries, $2,157 for expenses of the boarding department, $968 for repairs, and $640 for utilities. The remaining $579 was used to pay students for various tasks and for miscellaneous expenses.[9]

Von Tobel found the student body had grown slightly when he returned from North Dakota in the fall of 1914. Of 409 students, 28 were boarding on campus in dormitories maintained as Christian

---

[7] Raymond G. von Tobel, "Ballard School, Macon Georgia," *American Missionary* 67 (March 1914): 742–44.

[8] U.S. Department of the Interior, Bureau of Education, *Negro Education: A Study of the Private and Higher Schools for Colored People in the United States,* Bulletin No. 39, vol. 2, ed. Thomas Jesse Jones (Washington, D.C., 1916) 193–94.

[9] Ibid., 194.

homes. High school enrollment topped 150, making it the largest in several years.[10]

In the spring of 1917, Ballard Normal moved to its new facilities in a woodsy setting at the foot of a hill on Forest Avenue. Adjoining Macon's "finest colored residential section" were the new three-story school building, which bore a resemblance to the AMA's LeMoyne Institute in Memphis, a new teachers' home, and a caretaker's cottage. The up-to-date facilities included laboratories, sewing and domestic science and manual training rooms, a library that served the community as well as the school, and an auditorium capable of seating 600 people. For the first time, there was plenty of space for athletic activities. Despite the lack of adequate training facilities at the old site, Ballard had two baseball teams, a basketball team, and volleyball teams for both boys and girls.[11]

The AMA was greatly disappointed when, despite its modern facilities and spacious campus, Ballard enrollment began to drop. From a high of 417 in 1916, the year prior to relocation, enrollment fell to 359 in 1917, to 275 in 1918, and to 271 in 1919. One reason for the decline was the abandonment of the boarding department at the new campus. Although boarders had comprised a relatively small proportion of the student body, termination of the boarding department made an impact. (School officials continued to assist in securing housing with families in Macon for students.) The country's involvement in World War I may have been a factor, because after the war enrollments rose to 330 in 1921 and to 347 in 1922, but Ballard never regained its pre-war numbers. Despite low enrollments, von Tobel and his faculty never lost sight of their goal,

---

[10] *Catalogue of Ballard Normal School*, 1911–1912, 8–9; *65th Annual Report of the AMA*, 1911, 45–46.

[11] *Catalogue of Ballard Normal School*, 1911–1912; "After Seventeen Years," *American Missionary* 78 (December 1924): 347–49.

which was to deliver a well-rounded program of academic, vocational, and moral instruction to their students.[12]

The great threat to Ballard's enrollment was probably competing schools. In Macon, as generally throughout the South, public support for black education was increasing in the postwar years, due in part to efforts to halt the great migration of black laborers to the North. State and county officials in Southern states increased education funding for black students and attempted to appease African-American communities by providing better facilities and classes that extended beyond the sixth grade. Ballard's enrollment declined sharply after the opening of Hudson High and Industrial School, the city's first public high school for black students, in 1922, and Cressville Elementary School in 1923. Like Ballard, Hudson offered academic subjects as well as industrial education for boys and domestic science for girls. At Hudson, described by W. E. B. DuBois as "poorly constructed of the cheapest brick and wooden materials," most of the academic faculty held college degrees, and the industrial teachers were Tuskegee Institute graduates. In 1923, 127 teachers taught 5,554 black students in 16 public and private schools in Macon. The city's 9 elementary schools, one high school, and academy for the blind boasted an enrollment of 4,688 black pupils and a teaching staff of 92. Typically, as in Hazel Street Elementary School, a few teachers were college graduates while the majority had normal training.[13]

Private as well as public schools sprang up. Reverend Emanuel K. Love, president of the Missionary Baptist Convention in

[12] "After Seventeen Years," *American Missionary* 78 (December 1924): 347–48; *70th through 77th Annual Reports of the AMA*, pages for 1916, 45; 1917, 45; 1918, 43; 1919, 49; 1920, 49; 1921, 44; 1922, 42; 1923, 45.

[13] *Macon Telegraph*, 10 July 1929; W. T. B. Williams, "The South's Changing Attitude Toward Negro Education," *Southern Workman* 54 (September 1925): 398–400; W. E. B. DuBois, "The Negro Common School, Georgia," *Crisis*, vol. 32 (September 1926): 254–55. DuBois, throughout his years at Atlanta University, maintained a friendly relationship with von Tobel; for example, see letters of Raymond G. von Tobel to W. E. B. DuBois, 5 December 1924, and DuBois to von Tobel, 9 and 13 December 1924, NAACP papers.

Georgia, was the driving force behind Central City College, which offered elementary, secondary, and college classes for Afro Maconites. The school opened in 1920, but the building burned the next year. St. Peter Clavers School, a private elementary school operated by black Catholics, taught by two black and three white teachers, reported an enrollment of one hundred for 1922–1923. Minnie L. Smith, a former public normal school teacher, in 1921 used personal funds to establish (in honor of her sister) Beda Etta College, a private institution composed of grammar, normal, college, and commercial departments.[14]

Despite declining enrollments, academic standards at Ballard rose steadily, and in 1923 the state commission placed Ballard on the list of accredited high schools. That year, the number of accredited African-American high schools in the state jumped from two to ten, three of which—Ballard, Allen in Thomasville, and Knox in Athens—were supported by the AMA. The AMA eagerly sought accreditation for its schools and authorized whatever measures were needed to achieve it. Ballard lengthened its school year from thirty-three to thirty-six weeks and placed greater emphasis on high school development. As required by the state, three-fourths of Ballard's academic faculty were graduates of an accredited college or university, and the remaining teachers had the equivalent of two years of college or normal training, including at least twelve semester hours in the subject they taught. Principals had to show proof of college work in administration and supervision.[15]

---

[14] Donald L. Grant, *The Way It Was in the South: The Black Experience in Georgia*, ed. Jonathan Grant (Secaucus NJ: Carrol Publishing Group, 1993) 230.

[15] Raymond G. von Tobel, "After Seventeen Years," *American Missionary* 78 (December 1924): 348; *78th Annual Report of the AMA*, "The Accredited High Schools of Georgia," 8–9, 27; "Georgia State School Items: Certification," The State Department of Education: Atlanta, 10 (June, July, August 1923): 5, 10, von Tobel Papers; DuBois, "The Negro Common School," 251, 252, 263; Louis R. Harlan, *Separate and Unequal: Public School Campaigns and Racism in the Southern Seaboard States, 1901–1915* (Chapel Hill, 1958), see especially chapter 12 on Georgia: Public Schools and the Urban-Rural Conflict. See also Dorothy

Raising standards and meeting other requirements for accreditation increased expenses, and Afro Maconites responded to the need for additional funds with organizations such as the Ballard Willing Workers (BWW), organized in 1925 by a group of graduates and friends. That first year, the BWW paid tuition for twelve students, and a year later the group raised approximately $1,000.[16]

No doubt accreditation stimulated pride among Ballardites, but it also provided expanded opportunities for an interschool athletic program. Von Tobel encouraged competitive sports, not only for physical training but to teach "fair play" and "true conduct," and Ballard's program grew and flourished in the new location. When Ballard won its first state championship in high school basketball in 1925, there was pride among students and alumni alike.[17]

After accreditation, Ballard faculty also benefitted from closer contact with public school teachers. Ballard teachers began attending state teachers association meetings, and in the spring of 1926 the school hosted the conference. The convention met at Macon's Stewart AME Chapel, and Ballard teachers and their students mounted an impressive display of their abilities when they provided a luncheon for the visiting teachers.[18]

Von Tobel attempted further to enrich the Ballard educational experience by bringing in distinguished speakers to address the students and faculty. During 1926, Rev. Harold Vincent, a member of the Commission on Missions of the National Council of Congregational Churches, Frederick A. Sumner, president of Talledega College, and AMA Associate Secretary George N. White

---

Orr, *A History of Education in Georgia* (Chapel Hill: University of North Carolina Press, 1950) 329, and chapter 12 is especially helpful on black education in general during this period, as is the chapter on Politics of Education in Dittmer, *Black Georgia in the Progressive Era, 1900–1920.*

[16] *79th AMA Annual Report,* 1925, 16.

[17] Ibid.; "After Seventeen Years," *American Missionary* 78 (December 1924): 348.

[18] *80th AMA Annual Report,* 1926, 20.

spent time on campus talking with students and teachers. White also visited Hudson High and Beda Etta College. Chapel services featured talks by President Myron Winslow Adams of Atlanta University and Dean Samuel H. Archer of Morehouse College.[19]

After ending the 1926 school year on a positive note, minor tragedy struck during the summer while the teachers were on vacation. On 13 August 1926, daylight burglars broke into the teacher's home and stole $1,000 worth of equipment, including a piano, beds, chairs, dressers, dishes, and clothing. The burglars hauled away two loads of goods from eight rooms connected with the school and had bagged another load before arousing the suspicions of some members of the local black community.[20]

In spite of this and other setbacks, Ballard experienced general prosperity during the remaining years of the 1920s. Enrollments continued to rise, to 327 in fall of 1927 and 367 in 1928, and school tuition collections rose as well. Also during these years under von Tobel, race relations in the community improved dramatically. Ballard maintained its high educational standards and increased its extracurricular activities through the efforts of the AMA, outstanding auxiliary units such as the alumni and BWW, and, of course, the students. Students contributed toward the various AMA programs, raising as much as $250 for the annual Lincoln Offering to the AMA, as well as funds to purchase a film projector and fifty educational films and fifty dollars to purchase musical instruments for the school orchestra. Students also raised funds for new laboratory equipment and the installation of shower baths in the school basement. The orchestra raised additional money through various community engagements, mostly in local churches. Both the boys' and girls' glee clubs were invited to broadcast from local

[19] Von Tobel, "After Seventeen Years," 348; *78th AMA Annual Report*, 1924, 15–16, von Tobel Papers; *79th AMA Annual Report*, 1925, 16; *80th AMA Annual Report*, 1926, 20; Raymond G. von Tobel Diaries, 15, 18, 19 February 1926; 7, 10, 14 April 1926, Georgia State Archives, Atlanta, Georgia.

[20] "Daylight Burglars Steal Equipment of Normal School," *Macon Telegraph*, 13 August 1926.

station WMAZ. In dramatics, the junior and senior classes gave performances to which the community was invited.[21]

Rumblings of the approaching economic disaster were apparent by summer 1929. Local conditions reflected difficulties across the nation. The failure of summer crops in Bibb County was followed by the closing of the Fourth National Bank, one of the leading area banks patronized by blacks. Von Tobel noted the bank's closing and the seriousness of the situation in his diary. Heavy flooding compounded local problems and contributed to a slight decrease in fall 1929 enrollment, down to 315.[22]

These setbacks proved ominous, as the Depression brought even deeper yearly cuts in enrollment. However, throughout the Depression years, von Tobel remained optimistic and continued his diligent leadership of Ballard, encouraging students and teachers to maintain their usual high level of scholarship and achievement. Even as enrollments dropped, he continued to view the situation at Ballard with confidence and conveyed a sense of assurance to his superiors in the AMA. During stressful times he sought relief by leading teachers and friends on nature trips and birding hikes. Typical is an April 1931 newsletter piece in which von Tobel expressed his love of nature and his appreciation of the Georgia countryside:

> Peach-blossom time in middle Georgia! Acres upon acres and thousands upon thousands of peach trees in full bloom! I wish all our friends in the North could share with us this vision of surpassing beauty. Macon is only twenty miles from the heart of Georgia's peach belt, and we have just been viewing some of our largest orchards. Just imagine a vast mass of gorgeous pink

---

[21] *80th AMA Annual Report,* 1926, 20; *81st AMA Annual Report,* 1927, 22, 51; *82nd AMA Annual Report,* 1928, 13, 25, 26; *83rd AMA Annual Report,* 1929, 35.

[22] *82nd AMA Annual Report,* 1928, 26; *83rd AMA Annual Report,* 1929, 35, 75; von Tobel Diaries.

stretching away on either side of the road as far as the eye can reach... . Once seen, it is a sight never to be forgotten, and furnishes one of the thrills of a life-time. And as though this were not sufficient evidence of the arrival of Spring, our friend, the Meadowlark, is calling "Spring is here" as I write.[23]

In 1930, as in 1926, Ballard hosted the annual Georgia conference of Accredited High Schools and Colleges. Over fifty delegates from throughout the state attended various sessions, and, according to von Tobel, participants voted the conference the "best meeting ever." Once again, Ballard students from domestic science classes served a "sumptuous luncheon" they had prepared under the direction of their teachers. "Dining room and tables were attractively decorated, and in spite of a cold, rainy day everything inside radiated warmth and sunshine."[24]

While spirits remained good at the school, the economic hardship of the times was evident in fundraising efforts. Von Tobel was disappointed in the 1930 annual Lincoln Offering for the AMA: "Owing to the serious financial stress existing in this section at the present time the total, $163.43, was considerably less than last year." Nevertheless, von Tobel and all concerned recognized that the efforts "represented greater sacrifice and effort on the part of the students than ever before."[25]

Von Tobel appreciated the difficulties his students faced, as exemplified in his April 1931 newsletter mention of a "bright and intelligent" member of the class of 1930, battling the hardship brought on by the economic conditions of the country. "Through sheer determination coupled with a consuming ambition for an education she completed her high school course at Ballard." This young woman, he continued, planned to enter Talladega in the fall,

[23] Ballard Newsletter, 1 April 1931, AMAA; *83rd AMA Annual Report*, 1929, 5; von Tobel Diaries, 13 March 1926.

[24] Ballard Newsletter, 15 March 1930, AMAA.

[25] Ibid., 1930.

having earned tuition through housework and the care of a small child in the North. Von Tobel's report to the AMA noted that the "graduating class this year will be smaller than usual."[26]

With diminishing job opportunities for graduates during the Depression years, von Tobel and others felt that they might help students succeed by establishing a continuing relationship between new Ballard graduates and former students. Ballard clubs were organized in Northern industrial centers, including Chicago, Detroit, and New York, where, as in Macon, many Ballardites continued to advance in spite of the Depression. Two organizations, the Ballard Alumni Association and the BWW, also actively engaged in fundraising for the school. Projects such as a play given for the public titled "My Irish Rose" and an annual "Baby Show" were organized to raise scholarship funds.[27]

Macon's African-American community showed its support of Ballard in a number of ways. To help offset the loss in income from student tuition and to assist in solving the school's acute financial problems, black citizens of Macon called a meeting of leading black businessmen in the spring of 1931. They appointed a committee with a two-fold objective: first, to raise $1,000 by the close of the 1931 school term, and second, to conduct an intensive campaign during the summer months to increase fall enrollment substantially.[28]

During the Depression years, the Ballard Willing Workers' activities resulted in fewer dollars but greater city-wide participation. A 1933 alumni-sponsored "Miss Macon Contest" raised $100, while a "History of Ballard Pageant," written by alumni Raymond and Willis Pitts, managed a "good crowd" but only $34.85. Fortunately, AMA support remained strong; as tuition funds decreased, the association bore a greater share of the school's expenses. The 1930 annual report indicated that the AMA had

---

[26] Ballard Newsletter, 1 April 1931, AMAA.

[27] Ibid.

[28] *85th AMA Annual Report*, 1931, 33–34; Ballard Newsletter, 1 April 1931, AMAA.

extended to Ballard a total of $5,876.63; the following year the amount had increased to $8,060. In 1933 the AMA contribution was down somewhat to $6,511.[29]

That year, for the first time in Ballard's sixty-five years, an appeal for funds was made to the citizens of Macon. On 7 February 1933, the *Macon Telegraph* included an announcement that "Ballard Normal School, operated as a mission school by the Congregational Church and staffed by a white faculty is asking the public for help." The article, probably in von Tobel's words, went on to justify that request in terms of the white-black interaction Ballard exemplified:

> When the school was established here, there was a question in the minds of many citizens of Macon whether it would serve as a good purpose or not. That question has been answered to the entire satisfaction of everyone. The Board of Education has placed its approval upon the normal course of Ballard by selecting from its graduates most of the Negro faculty of our public schools. Its students have conducted themselves in exemplary manner. Whatever question there may have been in the mind of anyone about the desirability of a white faculty has been answered by the excellent work that the faculty has done in helping to adjust the Negro students to the white viewpoint. The school has served, indeed, a most useful purpose not only in the educational field, but also in the field of race relations.
>
> It deserves the commendation and the financial support of the city. Ordinarily it is supported by the missionary funds of the church and the tuition fees of

---

[29] *84th AMA Annual Report,* 1930; *85th AMA Annual Report,* 1931; *86th AMA Annual Report,* 1932; *87th AMA Annual Report,* 1933; Program, "The Story of Ballard," 5 May 1933.

students, but both have dropped this year. It would be tragic to lose the good work of the school.[30]

The Ballard Willing Workers sought to widen support of Ballard in its fundraising efforts for the 1933–1934 school year. As a means of reaching alumni in and around Macon, BWW president Mrs. Russell announced plans for a contest between the "Maids and Matrons" of the city to select "Miss Macon." The contest was held in conjunction with the annual Lincoln Drive. Von Tobel encouraged expanding the Lincoln Day activities to raise additional funds for the AMA, and the official drive was able to close the first week in March that year with a grand total of over $450. The particular aim for Ballardites during the Depression years was to raise sufficient funds from teachers, students, and black and white community friends to close out the school year free of debt. Ballard usually was successful in reaching its yearly goal. Since few people during these years were able to give more than a nickel or a dime, the annual sum collected represented not only a great number of individual contributors, but also much real sacrifice.[31]

Academic programs and standards remained strong through the Depression years, and students and faculty continued participating in various activities in the community and beyond, bringing pride to Ballard alumni and supporters. In 1931, for example, student China Birch won the Elks Oratorical Contest for Ballard in the state meet in Columbus. That same year, with Lewis H. Mounts as their adviser, Ballard students claimed leadership positions in the state council for Hi-Y activities. Overall, the school gained important recognition in 1934 when it was granted an "A" rating and full accreditation by the Southern Association of Colleges and High Schools, which included all the states of the

---

[30] *Macon Telegraph*, 17 February 1933, Washington Memorial Library, Macon, Georgia, Middle Georgia Archives, Ballard Normal School Collection.

[31] *Ballardite*, 13 November 1933, Washington Memorial Library, Macon, Georgia, Middle Georgia Archives, Ballard Normal School Collection; Ballard Newsletter, 15 March 1934, AMAA..

South and Southeast. That year's graduating class numbered forty-seven, almost back to the 1923 level.[32]

No doubt the accrediting association noted the quality of Ballard's teaching staff and principal, as evidenced by the ability of its graduates to gain acceptance to and succeed at various colleges and universities. A later statement by W. E. B. DuBois gives an impression of the kind of people with which the AMA staffed its Southern schools, including Ballard:

> This was the gift of New England to the freed Negro: not alms, but a friend; not cash, but character.... The teachers in these institutions came not to keep the Negroes in their place, but to raise them out of the defilement of the places where slavery had wallowed them. The colleges they funded were social settlements, homes where the best of the sons of the freedmen came in close and sympathetic touch with the best traditions of New England. They lived and ate together, studied and worked, hoped and harkened in the dawning light. In actual formal content their curriculum was doubtless "old-fashioned" but the educational power it gave was supreme, for it was the contact of living souls.[33]

And of the leadership of Principal von Tobel, one student wrote that "neither war, nor pestilence, nor the ravages of a Great Depression could destroy the dreams and hopes of a dedicated leader and principal as he struggled to shape the lives of young black men and women."[34]

---

[32] *85th AMA Annual Report*, 1931, 34; Ballard Newsletter, 15 March 1934, AMAA.

[33] Quoted in *Seeking a Way: A Partial Reprint of the Biennial Report of the American Missionary Association*, 1944.

[34] Raymond J. Pitts, *Reflections on a Cherished Past* (Reflections of the Ballard Norman School Experience by Graduates, with Commentary) 55.

Noted novelist and 1933 graduate John Oliver Killens later recalled the tough standards to which his teachers, including Helen Beeman, held their students. She assigned her ninth grade class an English composition, and several days later chose Killens' essay to read aloud in class. "I sat there bursting with pride," Killens wrote, "but alas it was the kind of pride that came before the fall." When she finished reading his "masterpiece," she told the class that she had read it as an example of what students should not do and accused him of copying it out of a book. "Needless to say, I was deeply hurt," Killens stated. "I could never convince her that I had not been guilty of plagiarism, though I can't remember that I tried very hard. Looking back, I can see that she was unintentionally paying me the ultimate compliment. I know I had not plagiarized it. She was sure that I had. It must have been pretty good."[35]

Another former student, Kathleen Cook Pitts, described the "faculty's determination to see that high standards of character and academic achievement [were] met, the faculty's unshakable faith in students' character, the faculty's constant encouragement of all students to reach far and to develop their potential fully." Even during the Depression years, Ballard graduates were encouraged to go on to college, and, by far, the majority of those who did chose education as their field of study.[36]

The standard four-year college-preparatory course at Ballard left students well prepared for higher studies. Each faculty member at Ballard had a specialty: Principal von Tobel taught sociology and civics, which were offered to eleventh and twelfth grade students; Lewis Mounts, assistant principal, taught Latin, history, and economics to ninth and tenth graders (ancient, medieval, modern, and U.S. history were offered after the ninth grade); B. T. Barrow taught biology and chemistry; Helen Foss taught English in grades nine and up, which constituted the high school, and also gave lessons in French; Ruth T. Holmes taught girls domestic science and domestic arts; and James Higgins taught manual training and

---

[35] Ibid.

[36] Ibid., 42, 44, 47.

mechanical drawing to the boys. (Below the ninth grade, courses in manual training were required for all boys and domestic arts and domestic science for all girls. In grades nine and up, advanced courses in these subjects were offered as electives.)[37]

In the 1930s, the lower grades at Ballard were organized and taught as a "practice school." Upper-level students in the normal course observed and taught these grades under the direction of their supervisor, who served as the department head. The seventh and eighth grades were organized as a junior high school. In addition to the standard academic courses, students took classes in agriculture, drawing, hygiene, and the New Testament.[38]

Monthly tuition at Ballard was based on grade level—the higher the grade, the higher the tuition. Typical fees between 1930 and 1935 were $2.50 for seventh and eighth graders and three dollars for high school students. Ballard also charged a special "graded" athletic fee, a nickel for the lower grades and fifteen cents for high school boys and a dime for high school girls. Students in the graduating class paid a one dollar diploma fee. Since Ballard was dependent primarily upon the American Missionary Association and student tuition fees for funds, its larger growth and development were made possible by gifts from alumni and friends, as described earlier.[39]

Outside the classroom, male students were encouraged to join the Hi-Y Club, which emphasized "clean thinking, clean speech, and clean living." Their symbol, the triangle, stood for body, mind, and spirit. School officials considered the club to be one of the most powerful forces for good in the lives of teenage boys at Ballard. The counterpart for girls was the Tri-Y. The clubs provided service in the greater Macon community, and under Mounts' direction students also participated in statewide Hi-Y and Tri-Y activities. The December 1933 *Ballardite* reported that the Tri-Y girls and Hi-Y boys responded to a call made in chapel just

---

[37] *Ballard Normal School Bulletin*, n.d., ca. 1930, von Tobel Papers.
[38] Ibid.
[39] Ibid.

before Thanksgiving and made up food packages for local needy families. "All loyal Ballardites truly feel that 'It's more blessed to give than to receive.' "[40]

Von Tobel summed up the influence of the clubs: "I think the intellectual, moral and spiritual level of our student body taken as a whole was never higher. Much credit for this improvement is due to the wholesome influence of our Boys' Hi-Y Club." All the teachers were engaged actively in Christian work. Students attended regular morning devotions, and tenth graders were required to take a course in Bible history. The religious activities were designed to hasten the spiritual life of the student body.[41]

Another important extracurricular activity, the student council, which involved students in policy-making and self-government, was instituted in 1928. Students were encouraged to discuss frankly methods of handling disciplinary matters and maintaining good behavior and neatness around the school. The school orchestra and an octet performed at schools and in churches throughout the city and did out-of-town engagements. The drama club generally performed two plays and one operetta annually. There was also a literary club, a bird study group, and a French club, Le Cercle, advised by Helen Foss.[42]

A Cammarian club was organized in 1928 to promote Christian ideals and to strengthen the school and uphold its high standards. Ballard's Cammarian Club was modeled after the one founded at Brown University, von Tobel's alma mater, and the clubs corresponded. Activities were wide-ranging: Club members helped new and out-of-town students adjust to the school and community, "fostered school spirit and student friendliness," and engaged in literary discussions of works by various writers past and

---

[40] Ballard Newsletter, 1 April 1932, AMAA; *Ballardite*, 13 October, 13 November, 20 December 1933.

[41] Pitts, *Reflections on a Cherished Past*, 42.

[42] *82nd AMA Annual Report*, 1928, 25; *Ballardite*, 28 November 1934.

present. The group frequently aided faculty members in remedying classroom problems.[43]

Athletic programs at Ballard were quite extensive. Grammar school students excelled in volleyball, while high school athletics generally thrived under science teacher B. T. Barrow. Football, basketball, baseball, and track teams competed successfully with local teams from Hudson High School, Central City College, and Beda Etta College. Barrow also took the teams to Cordele, Atlanta, Forsyth, Athens, Brunswick, Fort Valley, and Milledgeville. In 1932 Ballard won a state title in football and the city titles in football, basketball, and baseball.[44]

Under Raymond G. von Tobel's leadership, Ballard had moved relatively smoothly through the "boom" of the 1920s and the "bust" of the Depression and early 1930s. The school was entering another period of growth when, on 9 July 1935, von Tobel died after an automobile accident. Lewis Mounts became acting principal. The October 1935 issue of the *Ballardite* paid tribute to von Tobel: "How are the mighty fallen in the midst of battle. The beauty of Israel is slain in thy high places."[45]

---

[43] *Ballardite,* 20 December 1933.
[44] *Ballardite,* 13 October, 13 November, 20 December 1933.
[45] *Ballardite,* 29 October 1935.

CHAPTER 7

YEARS OF TRANSITION
1935–1949

The death of Raymond von Tobel, Ballard's beloved and forceful principal after a tenure of more than two decades shocked and dismayed Ballard and its supporters. In the months after von Tobel's death, unfounded rumors circulated that Ballard would close or at least cease to continue as an AMA school. Joseph Bailey, a school alumnus and employee, used the local press in an attempt to quiet these rumors. Bailey assured Afro Maconites that, as von Tobel had stated during his final commencement exercises in May 1935, "Ballard will open her 68th year of work to this community Sept. 13." Ballard "had already suffered too great a loss through the recent passing of the pri[n]cipal," Bailey continued, "and the numerous unpleasant rumors give room for doubt as to the security of Ballard's future." He reassured Ballardites that the "strength and capability of the great American Missionary Association" qualified its officers as "competent managers of AMA affairs," and urged supporters that "it would be wise to rest the matter to...intelligence and not to heard-hear-say-so." On the school's future, Bailey concluded, "Well wishers of Ballard hope that all unkind rumors will cease. None of us know. It is a wonder for us all. So, let us wonder and not rumor." Meanwhile, B. M. Russell, president of Ballard Willing Workers (BWW), released a statement to the local press that AMA Field Secretary George N. White had proclaimed that Ballard would reopen 13 September, as announced, under the acting principalship of Dr. Lewis L. Mounts.[1]

As might be expected, the search for a replacement for von Tobel was not an easy one. Students and faculty alike, however, "learned with great satisfaction" of the interim appointment of Mounts, a Ballard faculty member since 1914. The AMA home office in New York made it clear that Mounts was purely interim and that a permanent replacement would be sought. The May issue of the *Ballardite* applauded Mounts' appointment: "The fact that professor Mounts was a lover of the institution and a valuable asset to the late professor R. G. von Tobel in his beneficial and memorable works as principal, assured friends of Ballard that no one was any better qualified to carry on the work at Ballard than Mr. Mounts."[2]

Lewis Mounts, the eldest of three sons, was born in Monroe County, Iowa. He grew up in Moravia where he completed high school in 1907. He earned a bachelor's degree from the University of Iowa in 1911, and then master's (1914) and doctoral (1916) degrees in sociology and economics. Between his undergraduate and graduate work, he taught English for a year at Central Turkey College in Aincat, Turkey.[3]

Mounts, who went to Ballard in 1918, taught Latin, history, economics, religion, and sociology. He also had served as assistant principal and assistant director. He worked closely with the athletic program and had organized and advised Ballard's popular Hi-Y Club. Upon receiving his B.D. from Hartford Seminary in Hartford, Connecticut, he was ordained as a Congregational minister and pastored the First Congregational Church of Macon from 1920 until 1939. His wife, Berryl T. Mounts, also had studied at Iowa and had earned a Ph.D. in botany with a minor in

---

[1] "Ballard Rumors Unfounded," news clipping, n.d., ca. summer 1935; "Opening date Set By Macon School," n.d., ca. summer 1935, Ballard Collection, Washington Memorial Library, Macon, Georgia.

[2] *Ballardite*, 28 May 1936.

[3] Ibid.

paleontology. She held memberships in Sigma Xi National Scientific Honor Society, the American Association for the Advancement of Science, the Botanical Society of America, and the American Association of University Women.[4]

The 1935–1936 school year, under Mounts' leadership, was a period of transition for students and faculty alike. Ballard supporters, too, were grieved by von Tobel's tragic death, and the BWW undertook the task to commemorate the twenty-seven years he had served Ballard. First, the group took steps toward establishing a memorial fund to acquire books and to improve the general holdings of the school library, to be named the von Tobel Memorial Library. As von Tobel spent his life "helping mankind what would be a better memorial for him than one by which scores of seekers after knowledge at Ballard could be benefited," wrote the *Ballardite*. Each alumnus and friend of Ballard was asked to contribute one dollar toward the memorial. A bound volume containing the name of each person making a contribution would be placed in the library. Said the *Ballardite*, "Unborn generations in this manner will be able to read the names of the contributors to this most worthwhile purpose and Mr. von Tobel's life will ever be a living, glorious emblem by which boys and girls can pattern their lives." After the re-christening of the von Tobel Memorial Library, materials there were reorganized, useless articles discarded, and the cataloguing system rearranged. Within a year, the von Tobel Memorial Library contained 2,268 volumes, including reference books, fiction, magazines, and newspapers.[5]

Ballard was not the only institution undergoing changes. The AMA itself was in a state of transition. More and more AMA schools were being turned over to county boards of education, and

---

[4] Ibid. There is no mention of whether or not Berryl Mounts taught at Ballard.

[5] *Ballardite*, 28 May 1936; *Perplexing Realities: A Reprint from the Annual Report for 1937 of The Board of Home Missions of the Congregational and Christian Churches covering the work of The American Missionary Association Division from October 1, 1936 to May 31, 1937* (New York, 1937) 33; *Ballardite*, 27 May 1937.

AMA officials were urging Ballard and other affiliate schools to become more community-oriented, to find ways to bring the community and school closer. Unless AMA schools were somehow different than public schools, there was limited reason for them to exist. To facilitate this new thrust toward greater community involvement, AMA headquarters named Ruth A. Morton director of schools and community relations. Born in 1900 in Kansas City, Missouri, Morton was a 1929 graduate of the University of Denver and had received a master's degree from the University of Chicago Divinity School in 1934. Her first position with the AMA was as director of Lincoln Normal School, Marion, Alabama, after which she was appointed director of all the association's community schools.[6]

To increase its presence within the greater Macon community, the AMA developed plans to make Ballard a junior college. Acting principal Lewis Mounts first made this announcement in 1936 before details had been completed. The AMA solicited teachers qualified to teach courses in English, French, chemistry, biology, mathematics, social sciences, and teacher training. In general, junior colleges for African Americans tended to prepare students for jobs in home economics and normal training. Robert L. Cousins, Director of Negro Education for the Georgia Department of Education, visited Ballard and welcomed the new plan, provided courses outlined would meet the state's requirements for accreditation. The AMA already operated three junior colleges: LeMoyne Junior College, Memphis, Tennessee; Brick Junior College, Brick, North Carolina; and Tillotson College, Houston, Texas. The AMA concluded there was a need for such an institution in Central Georgia to provide further training for teachers and prospective teachers without certificates. Furthermore, many area black students were unable to meet the

---

[6] Edmund L. Drago, *Initiative, Paternalism, & Race Relations: Charleston's Avery Normal Institute* (Athens: University of Georgia Press, 1990) 199; *Facing Facts: A Review of the American Missionary Association's Eighty-Ninth Year 1935–1936* (New York, 1936) 14; *Perplexing Realities*, 33.

cost of a full college course of study outside Macon. A junior college at Ballard, by keeping its tuition fees low, could serve the needs of this population by offering regular courses and evening and Saturday extension work.[7]

The junior college proposal called for the elimination of primary and grammar school grades at Ballard, which thereafter would commence with eighth grade and extend through senior high and continue through junior college. By fixing tuition at a minimum rate, the new program was expected to aid hundreds of students locally and statewide by providing low-cost, high-quality higher education. Acting principal Mounts would serve as dean for the new junior college, with a new director to be named before fall 1936. The association's endorsement of a junior college met with an enthusiastic response from Macon's citizens. Supporters saw the dawning of a new era for black education in the city.[8]

On 8 September 1936 Ballard Normal opened its doors for a new fall term with a new director, Harwood Baldwin Catlin. Catlin adopted as the school's theme the winning slogan of a contest that had been held the previous spring. "A Past to Cherish, A Future to Fulfill" had been submitted by senior Mary Range, who had gone on to attend Talladega College in Alabama. As Catlin began his duties as Ballard's director, he followed the plan that had been outlined by AMA Secretary Fred Brownlee to recast Ballard to better serve the needs of the Macon community. The AMA sought to move toward activities that benefited the entire community, not just the "talented tenth." Catlin explained in the *Ballardite* that "the attempt will be made to preserve and extend the cultural values for which Ballard is so well known, while at the same time giving more attention to the five-sixths of the students who will probably not go on to higher education." Unfortunately for local students, the plan

---

[7] *Ballardite*, 28 May 1936; David A. Lane, "The Junior College Movement Among Negroes," *The Journal of Negro Education*, II (January 1933): 274–75, 283; Walter J. Greenleaf, *Junior Colleges, Bulletin, No. 3, United States Department of the Interior* (Washington, D.C.: Government Printing Office) 72–73.

[8] Ibid.

to turn Ballard into a junior college never materialized. Available records do not indicate why the plan was dropped.[9]

New director Catlin was born on 20 October 1891 near New London, Connecticut, at Fort Trumbull, where his father served as a field artillery officer. By age thirteen he had lived in six different states. After graduating from Franklin High in Hill, New Hampshire, he attended Harvard University and then the University of New Hampshire, graduating with a B.S. in 1912. He taught high school mathematics for three years before pursuing religious studies at Hartford Seminary, where he was a classmate of Lewis Mounts for two years before graduating in 1918. He studied for an additional year at Union Seminary, and then worked with the Interchurch World Movement surveying New England cities. In 1920 he and his wife, the former Laura Christeson, were commissioned to a South African Mission in Johannesburg; they returned to the United States in 1927. During the Depression years of 1931–1933, Catlin studied with Henry Hodgkin at the Quaker school at Pendle Hill, near Philadelphia, and at Yale University's graduate school of education. In 1934 he joined the faculty of Hampton Institute, Hampton, Virginia, as an associate professor of education, remaining there for two years before being appointed secretary of American Aid for Ethiopia, a voluntary organization to stimulate Red Cross support during the Italian invasion. The AMA believed that Catlin's international and multiracial experience would enable him to provide the leadership Ballard needed to effect more direct community involvement.[10]

Catlin's immediate goal was to improve the state of secondary education at Ballard, which he thought was inadequate and which could be properly provided only if students had the additional resources of a junior college. To address this concern, Catlin called a meeting of the entire faculty and local Ballard supporters. This group formed the Ballard Educational League (BEL). Catlin and

---

[9] Ballard Newsletter, 30 September 1936; *The Missionary Herald at Home and Abroad* 132 (September 1936): 414; *Ballardite*, n.d., November 1936.

[10] Ibid.

Dr. Mounts reported to the BEL on a recent conference at Marion, Alabama, for directors and executives of AMA secondary schools. The AMA desired more support from communities than it presently received, Catlin said, and with increased local support the association's appropriations could be expected to increase. Catlin commended the Macon community for the enthusiasm shown for a junior college, but cautioned the crowd that the city needed more accredited high schools and that more support from alumni and other supporters would have to be forthcoming before a junior college could be realized.[11]

Personnel changes also signaled a changeover from the "old guard" to the new ideas. Martha Ann Logan, eighth grade teacher for thirty-eight years, announced her retirement in the spring *Ballardite*. In the fall, Flora E. von Tobel and Elsie B. Tuttle, the librarian, announced their retirements. Students prepared a special fall issue of the *Ballardite*: "In appreciation of the loyalty and service rendered by these two loyal friends of Ballard Normal who are retired from the field of active service, we affectionately dedicate this issue." Another popular faculty member, mechanical arts instructor Henry Conklin, left Ballard to accept a position at the Choate School, Wallingford, Connecticut. The AMA accepted Conklin's recommendation for his replacement, Carlisle R. Saxton of New London, Connecticut, a 1935 graduate of the University of Vermont. Logan was replaced by Christina C. Mdodana, the daughter of a black South African minister and a graduate of North Carolina College for Negroes with a B.S. with high honors in mathematics. New courses in "Negro history" and commercial geography reflected modifications in the Ballard curriculum.[12]

In keeping with AMA objectives, Ballard expanded its community activities. Principal Catlin reported that Ballardites were making a special effort to serve the community and bring it closer with the school. Ballard became more involved in the Macon

---

[11] *Ballardite*, n.d., November 1936.
[12] Ballard Newsletter, 30 September 1936; *Ballardite*, n.d., November 1936; *Ballardite*, 28 May 1936.

community chest drive, the Red Cross drive, the sale of tuberculosis seals, and a fundraising effort for flood victims, and various faculty members contributed toward the equipping of a Girl's Reserve Club House.[13]

Unfortunately, after only one year, a heart condition compelled Catlin to leave Macon. As his replacement, the AMA selected Ballard's first black director since William A. L. Campbell in 1875. William Stewart Maize came to Ballard in September 1937 from Trenton, New Jersey. He was born and raised in nearby Rahway, where, while still in high school, he had worked distributing bakery goods and selling subscriptions to *The Crisis*, official organ of the NAACP, and the *New York Age*, a paper founded and edited by T. Thomas Fortune. To pay his tuition at Howard University, he and his cousin, William S. Nelson, who later became president of Dillard University, operated three newsstands. Maize graduated from Howard in 1922, and after a year of teaching school at New Bern, North Carolina, returned to Trenton to teach English at Lincoln Junior High. During summers he took classes at Columbia and Rutgers universities, and in 1933 he earned a M.Ed. from Rutgers. Before his appointment to Ballard, he had worked at the AMA's Tougaloo College, Tougaloo, Mississippi, for a year. Maize, as his predecessor Catlin, headed Ballard for only one year. The reason for his departure is not mentioned in AMA records.[14]

After three years of leadership changes at Ballard, the AMA selected another black director, James Allen Colston. A Floridian, Colston was educated in both primary and secondary public schools in Orlando. After high school he entered Morehouse College in Atlanta. A biology major and aspiring pre-medical student, he paid his tuition by mowing lawns and serving dinner at a Congregational home. Although his academic record was more

---

[13] *Perplexing Realities*, 33.

[14] *The Missionary Herald at Home and Abroad* 133 (August 1937): 357; Frederick D. Wilkinson, *Directory of Graduates Howard University 1870–1963* (Washington, D.C.: Howard University Press, 1965) 245.

than adequate for admission to medical school, Colston, discouraged by the high cost of medical training, settled on a career in
education instead. One of his teachers at Morehouse offered high
praise: "Colston was my best student and he would have made an
excellent physician, but a medical education is financially pro-
hibitive for most Negro young men." Colston returned to Florida
to serve five years as a high school principal in Deland. During this
time he managed to earn a master's in education from Atlanta University. Colston held important positions in the Florida State
Teachers Association, serving as a program director, district
president, Teacher's Credit Union president, and vice-president of
his county teachers' association. AMA Executive Secretary Fred
Brownlee believed that Colston could lead Ballard effectively
during its transition years: "He understands as only one who has
been a victim of segregation can understand. He has the courage
and wisdom and grace to proceed firmly, intelligently and tact-
fully." Colston was already familiar with the AMA. His wife was a
graduate of Talladega College and his sister taught at the AMA's
Fessenden Academy, Martin, Florida.[15]

On 14 June 1938, Ruth A. Morton informed Ballard personnel
of Colston's appointment. "We are very happy to tell you Mr.
James A. Colston of Ormond, Florida, has been appointed to the
Principalship of Ballard Normal School. Mr. Colston comes to us
with a fine background of training and experience.... Mr. Colston
will very quickly make his way into the hearts of both the teachers
at Ballard and the community folk." The AMA hired Colston
because it believed that he was the kind of person that Macon's
black community and Ballard needed to "lead the
way...concerning Ballard's future."[16]

---

[15] *The Missionary Herald at Home and Abroad* 134 (August 1938): 372–73.

[16] Ruth A. Morton to Willis N. Pitts, Myra I. Hardy, Fay S. Robinson, Lewis
H. Mounts, 14 June 1938, American Missionary Association Archives, Amistad
Research Center, Tulane University, New Orleans, Louisiana; hereafter cited as
AMAA. *A Continuing Service: A reprint from the Annual Report for 1938 of The
Board of Home Missions of the Congregational and Christian Churches covering the*

Colston assumed the helm at Ballard at a time when most parents outside of teaching and the skilled professions earned their living by doing odd jobs and domestic service. Since a large share of the school's operating expenses came from tuition and gifts, Ballard tended to be elitist at a time when the AMA sought greater community involvement. The association had already turned over all of its urban secondary schools to public authorities or fitted them into rural cooperatives, with the exception of Avery in Charleston and Ballard in Macon. Writing in *A Continuing Service* in 1938, Brownlee stated, "We are biding our time in Macon. We should not withdraw now and we ought not ever withdraw entirely. One of the big mistakes that the association has made down through the years and keeps on making is that it leaves cities and small communities when it withdraws from the school business on behalf of a public school." Brownlee continued, "Macon needs Ballard and the people out of their meager resources are paying a large share of the current expenses."[17]

Afro Maconites realized that in order to gain continued AMA support they had to make Ballard self-sustaining. With the AMA's encouragement, Colston held conferences with teachers, public school authorities, and members of the community to seek guidance as to how Ballard could better serve Central Georgia. He also met with the city school superintendent and with the state supervisor of Negro schools to seek cooperation with the city school system, as it was inevitable that eventually the public school system would assume responsibility for Ballard. Ballardites, too, met frequently to discuss these issues and school service in the future.[18]

---

work of *The American Missionary Association Division for the Year Ending 31 May 1938* (New York, 1938) 33–34.

[17] *A Continuing Service,* 34–35; Drago, *Charleston's Avery Institute,* 200–03. It should be noted that the author has not found evidence of a color caste at Ballard as Drago found at Avery.

[18] *Accelerating Social Evolution: A reprint from the Annual Report for 1939 of the Board of Home Missions of the Congregational and Christian Churches covering the work of The American Missionary Association Division for the Year Ending May*

During the mid-1930s, while Ballard was undergoing the turmoil of a constantly changing administration, a great impetus to increasing school enrollment and activities came through the National Youth Administration (NYA). A federally sponsored program begun in 1935, the National Youth Administration provided jobs to high school students through work-study programs. Some Ballardites participated in the program. Students were selected based on financial need but were required to demonstrate scholastic ability; to participate in NYA programs, students must have achieved a three-fourth passing rate. School officials planned projects for their students, and when certified by participating educational institutions, the federal government issued checks to the students.[19]

NYA programs covered a wide range of activities, which were grouped according to four major classifications: departmental assistance, construction and maintenance, clerical assistance and service, and semi-professional work. NYA participants worked as departmental or teacher's assistants, served as library aides repairing books, or did construction and maintenance work on campus, such as improving buildings, gymnasiums, playgrounds, and athletic fields. Still others served as clerical assistants doing general office work. Students received wages of from three to six dollars per month. Rates varied according to local wages for similar types of work, and students could not work more than four hours on school days and seven hours on non-school days. At Ballard, students could make application for NYA assistance directly through the principal's office.[20]

The Ballard NYA program was headed by a committee made up of director Catlin, Mrs. Catlin, Mrs. Mounts, Carlisle Saxton,

---

31, 1939 (New York, 1939) 15; *Bread and Molasses: A report from the Annual Report for 1940 of The Board of Home Missions of the Congregational and Christian Churches covering the work of The American Missionary Association Division For the Year Ending May 31, 1940* (New York, 1940) 17.

[19] *Youth, Jobs and Defense*, National Youth Administration (Washington, D.C.: Government Printing Office, 1941) 14–17, 24.

[20] Ibid.

and Joseph Bailey, the janitor. Four students, two boys and two girls, also served on the committee, one member each from the Hi-Y and Tri-Y and two NYA participants; the student committee was called Ballard's United Workers (BUW). Some of the NYA activities at Ballard were aimed at beautifying the campus through a "clean up campaign" and repairing books in the von Tobel Library. In 1936, NYA students, under Henry Conklin, built Ballard's first tennis courts (named the Conklin Courts). For months the "workers" labored, cleaning away bushes and trees to construct the courts. That year, NYA campus beautification projects and library work assisted more than sixty-five students at Ballard in paying tuition and fees. NYA money helped a number of out-of-county students to attend Ballard. The funds also enabled the school to employ Melvin Sikes, a trained band leader and a graduate of North Carolina College. Sikes organized a NYA band at Ballard upon his arrival in September 1940, and after only ten weeks the band performed before an assembly and even made recordings, which critics from the NYA called "remarkable."[21]

Colston expanded student activities at Ballard, and as a cultural center Ballard provided a variety of programs for both students and the community, especially in music and drama. To head the music program, Ballard was fortunate in attracting Aquilla Jones, a 1929 Spelman graduate with a degree in French. Jones had taken many courses under famed musician Kemper Harreld, head of Spelman's music department. She also had attended Chicago Music College and in 1932 earned a master's in music education from Columbia University Teachers College. According to Harreld, Jones was prepared to teach "beginners, intermediate and advanced students in piano, chorus and glee club, beginners violin, music history and appreciation, elementary theory and harmony." When she applied to Ballard, noted Spelman

---

[21] *Ballardite*, 27 May 1937; Ballard Newsletter, 21 September 1940; Ballard Newsletter, 30 September 1936; *Ballardite*, n.d., November 1936; *Ballardite*, 28 May 1936; Ballard Newsletter, 28 September 1936; *Bread and Molasses*, 17; American Missionary Association: Facts and Figures Form, 2 June 1942, AMAA.

president Florence M. Reed sent a letter in her behalf. At Ballard, Jones organized a choral class, a boy's glee club, an octet, and a girl's quartet and assumed the training of several soloists. The Kemper Harreld Music Club gained a good reputation in Central Georgia performing at both black and white churches in Macon and providing seasonal entertainment for local radio listeners.[22]

Dramatics had always been a favorite activity at Ballard, and it continued under the leadership of Willis N. Pitts, a Ballardite, 1925. Pitts saw to it that the school auditorium got long-needed equipment, and he directed the students in many popular plays such as "Who Did It," "Foot Steps," "LeLawala," "Betty, the Girl O' My Heart," and "Zippy." Several one- and three-act plays were produced each year by the school's dramatic club, and performances were enjoyed by the entire Macon community.[23]

The AMA and Ballard tried to do more for the community than simply providing cultural events. There were even efforts to make Ballard a genuine community center, to help with such needs as health services. Commencement themes reflected this initiative. For example, the spring 1939 focus was the "The High School and the Community," and Georgia educator Aaron Brown, dean of Fort Valley Normal and Industrial School (later president of Albany State College), delivered an address on "The Importance of Education for Community Development." Members of the graduating class presented a pageant titled "The High School Versus the Academic Curri[cu]lum." The following year the theme

[22] Florence M. Reed to the Board of Home Missions of the Congregational Churches, 19 November 1938, AMAA; Macon Telegraph, 29 November 1939; Music Program, " Aquilla Jones and Ophelia Taylor in Concert," 21 November 1938; Music Program, "Musicale," 29 November 1939; Music Program, "Josephine Harreld, Pianist," 24 April 1939; Music Program, "Rosalind Brown, Pianist," 19 May 1940; Ballard Newsletter, 6 October 1938, AMAA.

[23] Ballard Newsletter, 21 September 1940; Dramatic Program, "Who Did It," 17 April 1939; Dramatic Program, "Foot Steps," 15 April 1940; Dramatic Program, "LeLawala," 27 February 1939; Dramatic Program, "Betty, the Girl O' My Heart," 24 May 1939; Dramatic Program, "Zippy," 21 May 1940; Ballardite, 21 May 1940, AMAA.

was "The High School in American Society," and James O. Slade, director of the Division of Social Science, Morris Brown College, Atlanta, spoke on "The Responsibility of the High School in Community Development." That year, the graduating class pageant was called "American Society Versus the High School Graduate." As in the past, during these years many Ballard graduates were awarded scholarships to black Southern colleges.[24]

By the 1940s, efforts to increase community-based funding had been so successful that Ballard had become nearly self-sustaining. Yet, in 1942, after Ballard had raised $11,000 for its operations, the AMA announced a plan whereby Ballard would operate "no longer under the exclusive auspices of the American Missionary Association." The AMA asserted that because of tuition charges, Ballard was ministering to the "better-to-do group of Negroes." Therefore, beginning in fall 1942, the AMA had decided that Ballard would become a public cooperative school for black high school youth.[25]

The AMA would continue to pay the salaries of Colston and two teachers while the county paid the remainder. Unfortunately, Georgia's public school law prohibited mixed faculty, and Dr. Mounts and the other white teachers had to be retired. For the first time in Ballard's history the biracial faculty was abandoned. AMA officials considered Colston able enough to effect this transition from private to public school, saying, "Mr. Colston's excellent background and training, his high rating in the state of Georgia, and his splendid work during the past four years at Ballard have ably fitted him for this difficult position." The AMA insisted that it was not "withdrawing from the city of Macon." Colston would serve as liaison officer between AMA and city officials. The city planned eventually to erect a new school building and to turn

---

[24] *Accelerating Social Evolution*, 15–16; *Commencement Exercises Ballard Normal School*, 30 May 1939; *Commencement Exercises Ballard Normal School*, 28 May 1940; American Missionary: Facts and Figures Form, 2 June 1941.

[25] Fred L. Brownlee, *New Day Ascending* (Boston: Pilgrim Press, 1946) 139–40; American Missionary Association: Facts and Figures Form, 2 June 1941.

Ballard into a community center for Afro Maconites, but in the meantime, public officials would continue to use Ballard property as a school.[26]

When Colston unexpectedly resigned in 1943 to become president of Bethune Cookman College, Daytona Beach, Florida, it was a setback for both the AMA and Macon public school officials. The AMA appointed James Page of Avery Institute in South Carolina, a science teacher and assistant regional director of student work for the NYA. Page arrived at Ballard on 1 July 1943. A product of AMA schools, Page had graduated from Talladega College in 1931 and had received a master's from Columbia University Teachers College, 1935. Conditions were unfavorable as Page undertook his new position. By 1943 there was increasing unrest among black educators in Georgia and throughout the nation. A number of teachers were leaving to continue their schooling or because they no longer found teaching challenging or rewarding. Those entering the profession by this time held college degrees and felt they might seek opportunities outside teaching. At Ballard and in the Macon black community, many people wished for the school to continue as a private institution and hoped for the failure of the new cooperative arrangement.[27]

Unlike his predecessor, Page did not possess the personal or public relations skills to contend with the unrest among the Ballard staff or in Macon's black community. Before long, declining morale and increasing disciplinary problems prompted the local superintendent of schools to telegraph AMA headquarters about the chaotic situation at Ballard. Page claimed that the teachers were disrespecting him, which was creating the disciplinary problems. He later issued a statement on the state of affairs at Ballard in

---

[26] Ibid.; "Ballard School Enters Co-operative Program With Macon Board of Education," *Macon Telegraph*, 23 May 1942.

[27] Ruth A. Morton to Helen Wernert, 1 June 1943; Helen Wernert to James Page, 23 June 1943; James Page, Confidential Information File, the Board of Home Missions of the Congregational and Christian Churches, the American Missionary Association Division, AMAA.

which he urged supporters of the school to stop the whispering campaign, which was destroying school morale. A few days later, on 15 February 1944, Page wrote to Ruth Morton, who was planning a visit to Macon: "You will be just in time or perhaps a trifle late. I have been hesitant to write you, hoping things would blow over. The community is boiling and the principal is about to be fired. This is perhaps a trite way of expressing it, but for once I am lost for words. It has been a grand experience." Before he could be fired, Page resigned, and the AMA suggested that the Bibb County School Board hire the next principal.[28]

The board brought in Riago J. Martin, who had been employed as a principal for eight years in Waycross, Georgia, as the new principal. Martin related well to both parties and seemed to be the right person to head the kind of city high school the group envisioned. He played an important role as discussions continued between city and AMA officials about a new high school for blacks in Macon. City and AMA representatives worked hard together to plan a comprehensive high school for the city's black students. The group mapped out plans for the new school, to be named Ballard-Hudson. The school was created from a merger of Ballard, the AMA's first high school for blacks in Macon, and Hudson, the city's first black public high school. At the dedication in November 1949, city officials brought AMA Secretary Brownlee from New York to speak in addition to Dr. Aaron Brown and R. J. Martin. The Ballard-Hudson High School cost $2,500,000 and offered three courses of study: academic, vocational, and commercial. Vocational students could study brick masonry, carpentry, auto mechanics, commercial laundry, agriculture, and home economics. The school had modern, well-equipped science laboratories and classrooms and the auditorium seated 2,000. Ballard-Hudson High,

---

[28] James Page to Mark Smith, 13 February 1944; Western Union Telegraph, Mark Smith to Ruth Morton, 10 February 1944; James Page to Ruth Morton, 15 February 1944, AMAA.

which opened with a staff of fifty-five teachers and 1,200 students, was located in the black section of Macon, on Anthony Road.[29]

The AMA experience in Macon was about to come to an end. The years of contention between the Bibb County School Board and the AMA over providing and supporting first-rate schooling for Afro Maconites were honorably and happily concluded. Ballard-Hudson Senior High would provide a free education on an accredited level for all the high school pupils in the city. The AMA legacy would continue to be honored by the great and small achievements of many graduates.

---

[29] Brownlee, *New Day Ascending*, 140; Mark Smith to Ruth Morton, 3 January 1949; Mark Smith to Fred Brownlee, 12 July 1946; Mark Smith to Fred Brownlee, 24 January 1949; Mark Smith to Fred Brownlee, 28 January 1949; *Macon Telegraph*, 8 July 1949; *The Atlanta Journal*, 28 November 1948.

CHAPTER 8

CONCLUSION:
BALLARD ALUMNI

In 1911, alumnus W. E. Braswell wrote, "One of the best and surest means of determining the influence or usefulness of an educational institution is by the success or failure of its graduates." Judging by that standard, Ballard's achievement remained unquestionably positive. The school's approximately 3,000 graduates were well represented in a wide variety of trades and professions, from postal workers to university presidents. Even among its earliest graduates were those who stood as a living testimonial to the American Missionary Association and its contribution to African-American education in Central Georgia.[1]

One of Ballard's primary missions was to supply a sufficiency of African-American teachers for Macon and the surrounding counties. Other Ballardites became the businessmen and women of Macon and a majority of the physicians and dentists as well as the skilled artisans. These graduates were successful in their chosen professions and became leaders in their communities. Many Ballardites pursued further education at institutions of higher learning. Ballard graduates were well represented and represented Ballard well at Talladega, Atlanta, Fisk, Howard, Spelman, Morehouse, Hampton, Clark, Tuskegee, Morris Brown, and other

---

[1] *Catalogue Ballard Normal School,* 1911–1912; Raymond J. Pitts, *Reflections on a Cherished Past: Reflections of the Ballard Normal School Experiences by Graduates* (Macon: 1980), i. A great source of information for this chapter was Randall K. Burkett et al., eds., *Black Biography 1790–1950: A Cumulative Index,* 3 vols. (Alexandria VA: Chadwyck-Healey, 1991).

colleges and universities. After completing training in their chosen field, these men and women set out to "fill positions of large service to their race."[2]

Even some of the earliest students at both the Lincoln Free Schools and Lewis High School went on to college. Lucy Craft Laney, daughter of the Presbyterian minister David Laney, and William Sanders Scarborough went from the Lincoln Free Schools and Lewis High to the newly opened Atlanta University in 1869. Laney and Scarborough represented a small group of African Americans who had become literate in the antebellum South.[3]

On 23 June 1873, at Atlanta University's first graduation class, Laney received a teacher certificate from the Higher Normal Department.[4] Laney entered the teaching profession, and for the next ten years taught at various schools in Georgia—in Milledgeville, Savannah, and Augusta, as well as in her hometown of Macon. In 1883, with only five students, she rented a room in the basement of Christ Presbyterian Church of Augusta, and three years later she chartered the Haines Normal and Industrial Institute. By the end of the 1886–1887 school term, 234 students were enrolled. While serving as principal of Haines, Laney did graduate work at the University of Chicago and was awarded honorary degrees from Lincoln University in 1905, Atlanta University in 1923, and South Carolina College in 1925. Not only

---

[2] *American Missionary* 76 (December 1921): 416–17.

[3] Carter G. Woodson, *The Education of the Negro Prior to 1861* (Salem NH: Ayer, 1991) 211–12; William J. Simmons, *Men of Mark: Eminent, Progressive and Rising* (New York: Arno, 1968) 410–12.; Clarence A. Bacote, *The Story of Atlanta University: A Century of Service 1865–1965* (Atlanta: Atlanta University, 1969) 31–35; James D. Anderson, *The Education of Blacks in the South, 1860–1935* (Chapel Hill: University of North Carolina Press, 1988) 17; Thomas L. Webber, *Deep Like the Rivers: Education in the Slave Quarter Community 1831–1865* (New York: W. W. Norton, 1978) 131–38.

[4] Bacote, *The Story of Atlanta University*, 31–35; the higher normal course of study covered a wide range of subjects: arithmetic, algebra, geometry, geology, geography, botany, physiology, chemistry, physics, astronomy, literature, composition, history, civil government, Latin, review of English branches, mental philosophy, methods of teaching, and practice teaching.

was Laney a pioneer in African-American education, she played a significant role in the Women's Federated Club movement, the Inter-Racial Commission, and the National Association for the Advancement of Colored People (NAACP). Haines Normal and Industrial Institute, with some support from the Presbyterian Board, quickly expanded to include more than 900 students, with thirty-four teachers and a large physical plant. Before Laney's death in 1933, she saw the school become a junior college.[5]

William Scarborough also went from the Lincoln Free Schools and two years at Lewis High to Atlanta University. For the next two years he studied geometry, Latin, Greek, history, and civil government. From Atlanta he went to Oberlin College in Ohio, graduating in 1875, and obtained a master's degree from Oberlin Theological Seminary in 1878. After beginning his long teaching career at Albany Enterprise Academy, Albany, Ohio, he returned to Georgia, teaching first at Howard Normal at Cuthbert, then at his alma mater, Lewis High. He later taught Latin and Greek at Wilberforce University in Ohio, prior to becoming vice-president and then president there. Scarborough authored several books during the course of his distinguished career, among them the widely used *First Lessons in Greek* (1881), followed by a translation of Aristophanes' *The Birds* (1886), and *The Educated Negro and His Mission* (1903). As president of the Afro-American League he wrote scores of articles promoting the liberal and classical curriculum while denouncing vocational education as a viable option for blacks. He died in 1926.[6]

---

[5] Joseph J. Boris, *Who's Who in Colored America* (New York: Who's Who in Colored American Corporation, 1928–1929) 226; *Daily News*, 10 February 1934; "The Life and Times of Dr. Lucy Craft Laney," *Augusta News Review*, 27 May 1976; Bacote, *The Story of Atlanta University*, 408; Rayford W. Logan and Michael R. Winston, *Dictionary of American Negro Biography* (New York: W. W. Norton, 1978) 380.

[6] Simmons, *Men of Mark*, 413–18; *Macon Daily Telegraph*, 5 August 1901; Francis P. Weisenburger, "William Sanders Scarborough: Early Life and Years at Wilberforce," *Ohio History* 71 (1962): 209; Logan and Winston, *Dictionary of American Negro Biography*, 545–46.

Among the many other early Ballardites who became educators were Lincolnia C. Haynes, 1888, and William M. Hubbard, 1891, both of whom went on to Fisk. Haynes, valedictorian of her class, made her way through Fisk as a Jubilee Singer. She engaged in teaching and missionary work at her alma mater in Macon and later in Tennessee and Texas.[7] Hubbard began his career as a small-town teacher in Georgia. In 1900 he became superintendent at the AMA's Forsyth Normal and Industrial School at Forsyth, Georgia. Under his leadership, enrollment quickly grew to more than 500 and the school boasted a physical plant valued at over $15,000.[8]

Mack Primus Burley, 1902, received a B.A. from Atlanta University in 1908. He began his career as a photographer and teacher in Tattnall County, Georgia, before going to Alabama's Homer College, where he taught science, English, and Latin. He eventually became president of Miles College, Birmingham.[9] H. Sebastian Doyle, after leaving Ballard, obtained a B.A. from Clark University in Massachusetts and an M.A. from Ohio Wesleyan. He later received the Doctor of Divinity degree and pastored important churches in Birmingham, Washington, D.C., Augusta, and Shreveport.[10]

Ballardite Charles J. Johnson joined a small emerging class of black professionals in Central Georgia. He entered Walden University (formerly Central Tennessee College) at Nashville,

---

[7] *Catalogue Ballard Normal School*, 29; J. B. T. Marsh, *The Story of The Jubilee Singers Including Their Songs* (London: Hodder and Stoughton, 1897) 109–10.

[8] A. B. Caldwell, *History of the American Negro and His Institutions*, Georgia Edition (Atlanta: A. B. Caldwell, 1912) 562–64; *American Missionary* 58 (February 1904): 35; *American Missionary* 56 (July 1902): 329–30.

[9] *Catalogue Ballard Normal School*, 1911–1912, 31; *Who's Who of the Colored Race*, 1915, ed. Frank L. Mather, vol. 1, (Detroit: Gale Research, 1976) 51; Bacote, *The Story of Atlanta University*, 410.

[10] *Official Program and Music of the Negro Young Peoples' Christian and Educational Congress*, 31 July–5 August 1906 (Washington, D.C.: I. Garland Penn) 75.

exiting with a B.A. in 1899. Johnson earned a law degree in 1913 from Howard University Law School in Washington, D.C., and then practiced law in Kentucky before returning to practice in Macon. An active member of the community, Johnson served as secretary of the local Young Men's Christian Association (YMCA) and as steward, trustee, Sunday school teacher, and superintendent of his church. When black Maconites observed the Emancipation Day Celebration on 1 January 1910, Johnson delivered a speech titled "The Pilgrimage of a Race," which was published in pamphlet form.[11]

Walter Reid went from Ballard to Johnson C. Smith University, Charlotte, where he received a B.A. in 1889. Returning to his hometown of Macon, where he was letter carrier for thirty-one years, Reid served as grand chancellor of the Knights of Pythias, president of the Business League of Macon, and chairman of the board of directors of Middle Georgia Savings and Investment Company.[12]

After attending Lewis High and Haines Normal and Industrial Institute, Jose Henry Sherwood migrated north to St. Paul, Minnesota. He headed the postal service of that city and became active in his community through his association with various orders of the masonry.[13] Other Ballardites who worked as postal clerks in various cities included Charlie Ross, 1883, Philadelphia; William Hill, 1891, Macon; Charles Taylor, 1907, Augusta; and Lain Parks, 1909, Macon.[14]

A large number of Ballard graduates worked in the insurance business in various cities: William Matthews, 1883, in Atlanta, and Clarence M. Robinson, 1886, Asa Ashley, 1901, and Abram McKissick, 1902, in Macon. Truman Gibson, class of 1900, earned B.A. degrees from Atlanta University in 1905 and from Harvard in

---

[11] Caldwell, *History of the American Negro*, 58–61.
[12] Boris, *Who's Who in Colored America*, 1928–1929, 304; Thomas Yenser, *Who's Who in Colored America*, 1941–1944 (Brooklyn: Yenser, 1944) 433.
[13] Yenser, *Who's Who in Colored America*, 1941–1944, 462.
[14] *Catalogue Ballard Normal School*, 29, 33, 34.

1908. Gibson taught at the St. Paul School, Lawrenceville, Virginia, before entering the insurance field. He served as secretary and vice-president of Atlanta Mutual Insurance Company of Atlanta and as secretary of Atlanta Loan and Trust Company. When the Supreme Life and Casualty Company of Ohio debuted in 1919, Truman Gibson was a driving force in that organization. Later, when it had become the Supreme Liberty Life Insurance of Chicago, Gibson served as chairman-treasurer. For his long and dedicated service to the industry, he was awarded the prestigious Harmon Medal, awarded in 1930.[15]

Among those early graduates who put their skills to work to become entrepreneurs were tailors Eugene Thompson, 1882, in Philadelphia; Frank H. Weaver, 1889, in Atlanta; and Thomas Jones, 1883, who eventually headed the Tailoring Department at Tuskegee; and seamstresses Louise Brooks (Douglas), 1891, Mamie Lafitte (Clay), 1901, and Mabel Smith, 1903, all of Macon.[16]

Sidney David Williams, 1909, received a B.A. from Atlanta University in 1914, and an M.S. sixteen years later from Teachers College of Columbia University. He was athletic director at Bluefield Institute, West Virginia, and at Johnson C. Smith, and later served as both dean and president at State Teachers College, Elizabeth City, North Carolina.[17]

Ballardite Thomas Solomon Kemp earned a B.A from Talladega in 1908 and did further study at Columbia University and the University of Pennsylvania. Kemp managed the Industrial Orphanage Home, Columbia, South Carolina, served as teacher

---

[15] *Catalogue of Ballard Normal School*, 29–35; Mather, *Who's Who of the Colored Race*, 1915, 115; Yenser, *Who's Who in Colored America*, 1941–1944, 205.; M. S. Stuart, *An Economic Detour: A History of Insurance in the Lives of American Negroes* (New York: Wendell Malliet, 1940) 84–86. Bacote, *The Story of Atlanta University*, 142, 197, 211.

[16] *Catalogue Ballard Normal School*, 29–35.

[17] G. James Fleming and Christian E. Burckel, *Who's Who in Colored America*, 7th ed. (New York: Christian E. Burckel and Associates, 1950) 562.

and academic director of Voorhees School, Denmark, South Carolina, and later directed the YMCA as executive secretary.[18]

Architect W. Augustus Rayfield attended both the intermediate and high school divisions of Ballard before going on to Howard University to study Classics; he graduated in 1896. He went on to study architecture at Pratt Polytechnic Institute in Brooklyn, New York, and at Columbia University (B.A., 1899). At Columbia, Rayfield met Booker T. Washington, who invited him to join the faculty at Tuskegee. He taught mechanical and architectural drawing there for nearly a decade. Later, Rayfield practiced his profession in Birmingham and eventually became the official architect for the Zion A.M.E. Church, in charge of all planning for new churches. He also designed the schools for the Freedmen's Aid Society headquartered at Cincinnati.[19]

Two early Ballardites, William Braswell, 1891, and Junius Bell, 1904, both of Macon, became dentists. Braswell completed his dental training at Meharry Medical College and at Walden University, both in Nashville, in 1910. He practiced briefly in Macon before moving to Atlantic City, New Jersey. A few years later Leola Hubbard, 1911, completed medical training at Meharry.[20]

Several of the many Ballardites who pursued higher education became distinguished professors. Catherine Mae Hawes, after completing her B.A. at Atlanta University in 1908, continued her studies at the University of Chicago and the International People's College of Elsinore in Denmark. She headed the math department at Tennessee Agriculture and Industrial State College of Nashville before serving as field secretary of the New York City YWCA from 1920 to 1924. While in New York, she attended Columbia University Teachers College, receiving an M.A. in 1926. Hawes

---

[18] Ibid., 323.

[19] Green P. Hamilton, *Beacon Lights of the Race* (Memphis: E. H. Clarke and Brother, 1911) 452–57.

[20] *Catalogue Ballard Normal School*, 30, 32, 35; Mather, *Who's Who of the Colored Race*, 1915, 36.

later worked as head of the department of social sciences at
Bethune-Cookman College, Daytona Beach, Florida (1948–1949),
and as dean of women at Cheyney State College, Cheyney,
Pennsylvania. Hawes published numerous articles on adult
education.[21]

Samuel Milton Nabrit went from Ballard to Morehouse
College in Atlanta, where he received his B.S. in 1925, on to Brown
University in Providence, Rhode Island, to complete the M.S. and
Ph.D. degrees in biology in 1928 and 1932, respectively. In 1932 he
was the first professor hired by Atlanta University for its new
biology department. Under Nabrit's leadership, the department
became one of the strongest at the university, and in 1947 he was
named dean of the Graduate School of Arts and Sciences. In 1955
he assumed the presidency of Texas Southern University. Nabrit
was published in several scientific journals.[22]

Another prominent Ballardite was Brailsford Reese Brazil, who
received a B.A. from Morehouse College in 1927 and an M.A. and
Ph.D in economics from Columbia University in 1928 and 1942,
respectively. His dissertation, "The Origin and Development of the
Brotherhood of Sleeping Car Porters," was published later by
Harper. Brazil taught at Morehouse College before serving as
chairman of the department of economics and later as dean of
men, with a dual appointment during 1934–1947. Brazil made

---

[21] Fleming and Burckel, *Who's Who in Colored America*, 1950, 602. Hawes'
publications included "Community Experiment in Adult Education" in the
Journal of the National Association of College Women (1934) and "The Inter-
relationship of Colleges and Community Agencies in Promoting Adult
Education" in *Report of the Annual Meeting of Negro Presidents of Land Grant
Colleges* (1942).

[22] Vera Chandler Foster and W. Hardin Hughes, *Negro Year Book
1941–1946* (Alabama: Tuskegee, 1946) 35; Harry Washington Greene, *Holders of
Doctorates Among American Negroes* (Boston: Meador Publishing Co., 1946) 194;
Bacote, *The Story of Atlanta University*, 286–87. Nabrit's publications included
excerpts from his dissertation on "Regeneration in Tail-fins of Fishes."

occasional contributions to *Phylon*, the *Journal of Negro Education*, and the *Quarterly Review of Higher Education Among Negroes*.[23]

Although Ballard provided, on the average, approximately ninety percent of all Central Georgia educators, many teachers joined the great migration northward. Some of those were Cleopatra Love, 1910, a high school teacher who attended Fisk, Atlanta, and New York universities; Mae McElmurry Miller, 1917, elementary teacher who attended Tuskegee, Atlanta University, Fort Valley State College (B.A.), and New York University (M.A.), and studied piano, voice, and organ at Detroit Conservatory of Music; Annie Mae Gaston Tillman, 1917, who was admitted to the Chicago Hall of Fame for her leadership in Chicago's Head Start program; Bessie Grier Watson, 1917, elementary teacher, Detroit, who received teacher training at Penn School in South Carolina; Julia B. Jackson Crew, 1918, elementary teacher, Detroit, who trained further at Cheyney State College, Tuskegee, and Kalamazoo State Teachers College in Michigan; Rosetta Smith, 1922, elementary teacher who studied at Fort Valley State College; and Theodora Williams, 1927, high school teacher who studied at Howard University (B.A. 1931, M.A. 1937), Boston University, Catholic University in Washington, D.C., and at Yale University as a John Hay Whitney Fellow and as the Agnes and Eugene Meyer Fellow for Study and Travel in Europe.[24]

Albert C. Howard, 1928, industrial arts teacher, went on to Morehouse (B.A.), Savannah State College, and the University of Georgia. Carolyn Walker Pitts, 1930, elementary teacher, studied at Fort Valley State (B.S.), New York University (M.A.), and the University of Los Angeles. Kathleen Cook Pitts, 1930, who taught both at the elementary and secondary levels, received extensive training at Talladega (B.A.), Georgia State College in Savannah, Atlanta University, University of Michigan in Ann Arbor, Howard

---

[23] Greene, *Holders of Doctorates Among American Negroes*, 51; Fleming and Burckel, *Who's Who in Colored America*, 1950, 51.

[24] Pitts, *Reflections on a Cherished Past*, 15, 17, 18, 24, 34.

University, and California State University, University of California, and Pepperdine University, all in Los Angeles.[25]

Robert F. Jackson, 1931, elementary school principal, attended Morris Brown College, Atlanta University, and the University of Georgia. Naomi Lucas Cheatham, 1932, attended Talladega (B.A) and then Temple University (M.Ed.) in Philadelphia, where she worked as a high school counselor. Lois White Lane, 1932, obtained a B.S. from Fort Valley State College and an M.A. from Atlanta University, held positions as both teacher and Jeanes supervisor. Elizabeth Lother Jones, 1935, teacher and registrar, trained at Fort Valley State College, Teachers College of Columbia University, Atlanta University, Mercer University, and the University of Georgia.[26]

Annie Ruth Cornelius Campbell, 1938, a school media specialist, attended Talladega College, Atlanta University, University of Michigan, and Florida State University. Sarah Calhoun Mclendis, 1941, elementary teacher, was one of the first two black women to obtain a master's degree from Mercer University in Macon. Leonard Summers, 1941, elementary school principal, studied at Morris Brown College (A.B.), Atlanta University School of Social Work (MSW), Florida A&M University, and University of South Florida. Robert J. Williams, 1942, who worked a number of years as a school superintendent in Macon, studied at Morehouse (B.A.) and Atlanta University (M.A. and Ed.D).[27]

A number of Ballardites made a strong contribution in the area of social welfare, both at home in Macon and in the North. Maconite Martha Williams Sheftall, 1923, trained at Fisk (B.A.), Columbia University, and Fort Valley State. After receiving a B.A. at Wayne State University in Detroit, Gladys Smith Scott, 1925, became a social worker in that city. Willis B. Sheftall, 1926, returned to Macon after attending Lincoln University (B.A.) in Pennsylvania and Atlanta University. The *Macon Telegraph* cited

---

[25] Ibid., 37, 46, 47.
[26] Ibid., 48, 50, 51, 67.
[27] Ibid., 73, 85, 88, 90.

Sheftall for more than forty years of service to the Macon community: "He is goal oriented and if he sets a goal, he does everything in his power to attain that goal...it was his desire to give something back to his home town."[28]

Violetta Ming Lee, 1934, continued in the missionary tradition after furthering her schooling at Fort Valley State College and Tuskegee Institute. She was a social worker in Baltimore, where she also attended Coppin State. Charles Holmes, 1936, became a psychiatric social worker in Brooklyn, New York, after extensive preparation at Brooklyn College and Fordham University School of Social Service, New York Center for Psychoanalytic Training, Beth Israel Hospital Department of Psychiatry, New York School of Social Work, and the Spanish Institute, all in New York City. Ruby Clowers Sulton, 1941, a social worker in Orangeburg, South Carolina, studied at Atlanta University School of Social Work (MSW) and Wayne State and Duke universities.[29]

A few Ballardites became librarians. Eva Phillips Lee, 1927, had a distinguished dual career as teacher and librarian in Macon after attending Fort Valley State College (B.S.) and Atlanta University (M.S.L.S.). Dorothy Cooper Bonner, 1933, studied at Paine College, Augusta, and at Tuskegee Institute, Fort Valley State College, and the University of Georgia. Miriam Reese Spence, 1943, took the B.S.L.S. from Florida A&M University and the M.S. from Troy State University in Alabama.[30]

Despite facing the limitations posed by racial barriers, a number of Ballard graduates went on to gain national and, in some cases, international prominence. Asa Gordon, 1910, became a college professor, dean, and author. He attended Atlanta University (B.A., 1917), Hamilton College of Law in Chicago (LL.B., 1920), Columbia University (M.A., 1932), Harvard University, and the University of Minnesota. Gordon served as field agent for the department of sociology at Atlanta University in 1917 and

---

[28] Ibid., 26, 31, 33.
[29] Ibid., 60, 69, 84.
[30] Ibid., 36, 51, 93.

educational secretary for the army YMCA, Camp Gordon, Georgia, in 1918. He taught in the history department at South Carolina State College (1918–1927) and served as dean (1928–1936) and later as director of research and publications (1939–1942) at Georgia State Industrial College in Savannah. Gordon also taught at Southern University in Baton Rouge, Louisiana, Delaware State College, and Alcorn A&M College in Alcorn, Mississippi. He published several works during his career, including *Sketches of Negro Life and History in South Carolina* (1929) and *The Georgia Negro: A History* (1937).[31]

Celestine Louise Smith, 1921, who distinguished herself in the field of social work and counseling, studied at Talladega College (B.S., 1925), the University of Southern California (Certificate in Social Work, 1942), and Teachers College of Columbia University (Ed.D., 1952). Smith also received training in psychological analysis at Union Theological Seminary in New York and University of Chicago Divinity School. After teaching for two years at a private high school in Alabama, she joined the staff of the Young Women's Christian Association (YWCA) in 1929 and remained until 1968. She served in a number of capacities, including national student secretary in the Southwest, director of counseling and case work, and as a specialist in human relations. She also spent one year as director of the YWCA in Lagos, Nigeria. Throughout her career with the YWCA, Smith worked to improve race relations and to desegregate public institutions.[32]

Lawyer and statesman Ernest Greene, 1919, studied at Talladega College (B.A., 1923) and at Chicago's Kent College of Law (LL.B., 1930). He was admitted to the Illinois Bar in 1931. In 1936 Greene was elected to the Illinois General Assembly; he was

---

[31] Fleming and Burckel, *Who's Who in Colored America*, 1950, 217–18; Asa H. Gordon, *The Georgia Negro: A History* (Spartanburg SC: Reprint Co., 1972) 390.

[32] Darlene Clark Hine, ed., *Black Women in America: An Historical Encyclopedia*, vol. 2 (Brooklyn: Carlson, 1993) 1078; *New York Times*, 19 December 1975, 42.

reelected in 1938, 1940, and 1942. He was a partner in the law firm of Brown, Brown, Cyrus and Greene.[33]

Thomas Ralph Solomon, 1923, an educator and activist, attended Wayne State University (B.A., 1929; M.A., 1933) and later studied political science at the University of Michigan (Ph.D., 1939). His dissertation was titled "Participation of Negroes in Detroit Elections, 1929–1933." Solomon became an outstanding member of the faculty of Prairie View State College in Texas. He was decorated by the Liberian government in 1961 as "Knight Commander of the Humane Order of African Redemption" for distinguished service and leadership in the development of educational programs at the Booker T. Washington Agricultural and Industrial Institute at Kakata, Liberia.[34]

Ballardite Julia Carey Fitzpatrick, 1924, distinguished herself as an outstanding club leader. After attending Tuskegee Institute, she held positions as National Grand Matron and secretary-treasurer of the National Masonic Charity and Relief Department and vice-president of the Federation of Eastern Stars. She also held leadership posts in both the National Council of Negro Women and the National Association of Colored Women.[35]

Ballard educated several generations of some Macon families. One was the Coleman-Killens family. William O. Coleman finished old Lewis High before 1888, and was followed by his daughters Willie Coleman Killens and Louise Coleman Ketch, Ballard 1911 and 1913, respectively. Willie's children, Charles M. Killens, Jr., 1931; John Oliver Killens, 1933, and Richard Leo Killens, 1937, followed in the family footsteps. Willie Killens taught for several years in the Macon public schools before joining the Atlanta Life Insurance Company, where she remained for twenty-one years. She

---

[33] Edward J. Hughes, ed., *Blue Book of the State of Illinois*, 1943–1944 (Springfield IL: Department of State, 1944) 366; Charles F. Carpentier, ed., *Illinois Blue Book* 1955–1956 (Springfield IL: Department of State, 1956) 202.

[34] Greene, *Holders of Doctorates*, 264; Fleming and Burckel, *Who's Who in Colored America*, 480; article in *Macon Telegraph*, 1949 (n.d., n.p.).

[35] William C. Matney, *Who's Who Among Black Americans* (Northbrook IL: Who's Who Among Black Americans, 1975–1976) 203.

later joined her sons in Washington, D.C., working there as recorder of deeds for the U.S. Navy Bureau of Ships, Saving Bonds Division of the U.S. Treasury, and the Library of Congress.[36]

Charles M. Killens, Jr., took business administration at Morris Brown College (B.A., 1935), after which he worked briefly as a traveling representative for Atlanta Life Insurance Company. In 1936, he began work in Washington, D.C., with the U.S. Government Printing Office as a printing operative. He served in the armed services during World War II, after which he resumed his career, working as editor of the Government Printing Office Style Manual and as head proofreader for government publications.[37]

Perhaps the most distinguished twentieth-century graduate of Ballard Normal was John Oliver Killens, writer, teacher, and a founder of the Harlem Writers Guild. In addition to studying at three historically black colleges, Edward Waters, Morris Brown, and Howard (where he got his degree), he also studied at Terrell Law School, Columbia University, and New York University. Killens taught creative writing at various colleges and universities, including Fisk, Howard, Columbia, and Medgar Evers College. As a member of the Harlem Writers Guild, he spent much of his career tutoring and nurturing young would-be writers, among them Maya Angelou, Nikki Giovanni, Richard Perry, Arthur Flowers, Douglas Turner Ward, John Henry Clark, Lonne Elder III, Paule Marshall, and Sarah Wright.[38]

Killens's first novel, *Youngblood* (1954), revolved around the life of an African-American family in a small Georgia town. His next, *And Then We Heard the Thunder* (1963), which focused on the racist policies of the U.S. military during World War II, was nominated for the Pulitzer Prize in 1964. His other writings include

---

[36] Willie Coleman Killens to Raymond J. Pitts, 27 January 1980, American Missionary Association Archives, Addendum. Hereafter cited AMAA.

[37] Charles M. Killens to Raymond J. Pitts, 24 January 1980, AMAA.

[38] John Oliver Killens to Raymond J. Pitts, January 1980 (n.d.), AMAA; *New York Times*, 30 October 1987, 22.

Sippi (1967), the story of an African-American family in Mississippi; *Cotillion: Or One Good Bull Is Half the Herd* (1971); *Great Gettin' Up Morning: A Biography of Denmark Vesey* (1972); and a children's book, *A Man Ain't Nothin but a Man: The Adventures of John Henry* (1975).[39]

Another set of brothers, the Pitts, also made their way through Ballard. Brothers Willis N., 1925, Robert B., 1926, Raymond J., 1928, and Nathan A. Pitts, 1931, all had distinguished careers. Willis Pitts, a university professor and speech pathologist, attended Talladega (B.A.), University of Michigan (M.A. and Ph.D.), and did postdoctoral work in speech pathology at Boston University.[40]

Robert Pitts, a well-known economist and urban consultant, studied at Howard University (B.S., 1938), University of Washington at Seattle (M.A., 1941), University of California at Berkeley, and the Brookings Institute (advanced study in public administration). Howard University awarded him the distinguished service award for his contributions toward the development of a model community. He also was recognized for his involvement with the U.A.W. (AFL-CIO). He served as race relations officer for San Francisco's public housing authority and worked for the city of Seattle as a statistician.[41]

After receiving degrees from Talladega College (B.A.) and the University of Michigan (M.A., Ph.D.), Raymond Pitts had a long and distinguished career as an educator and administrator. He taught at schools in Georgia and Florida before accepting a position at Fort Valley State College, where he taught for eighteen years and introduced the first All-State Science Fair in Georgia. After moving to California he taught at Los Angeles State College and directed the Center for Coordinated Studies at Santa Barbara. He also served as president of the National Institute of Science, 1955–1956. During the latter part of his career he was a member of

---

[39] *New York Times*, 30 October 1987, 22.

[40] Raymond J. Pitts, *Reflections on a Cherished Past*, 30.

[41] Fleming and Burckel, *Who's Who in Colored America*, 419; *Who's Who in the West*, 11th ed. (Chicago: Marquis, 1975) 546.

the chancellor's staff, serving in the capacity of dean of academic affairs for California community colleges.[42]

The youngest brother, Nathan Pitts, had a dual career as a university professor and a government administrator. He studied at Florida A&M University, Xavier University of Louisiana, New Orleans (B.S.), Catholic University of America (M.A., Ph.D.), and at Harvard, Boston University, and Johns Hopkins. Pitts began as an instructor at North Carolina College in Durham and later became chairman of the division of social sciences at Shaw University, Raleigh, North Carolina. The author of *The Cooperative Movement in Negro Communities of North Carolina* (1950), he ended his career as an administrator for the federal government.[43]

Captain Pierce B. Brunson, 1934, an elementary school teacher and principal, distinguished himself in the U.S. Army. He completed his B.S. at Morris Brown College in social studies in 1938 and the master's in education from Atlanta University. Following graduation, Brunson worked as a teacher in Austell, Georgia, before briefly joining Pilgrim Life Insurance Company. He entered the armed service at the beginning of World War II, and in 1944 was commissioned as second lieutenant in the transportation corps at Brisbane, Australia. After the war, Captain Brunson taught for many years at the new Ballard-Hudson School before becoming principal of Maude C. Pye Elementary School in Macon.[44]

Mattie Jewel May Davis, 1930, earned honors for her civil rights and community work. Following graduation from Ballard she became an apprentice cashier-clerk for North Carolina Mutual Life Insurance Company. In 1942 she entered the civil service and remained for eighteen years. In 1977 she was nominated as one of

[42] Vivian Ovelton Sammons, *Blacks in Science and Medicine* (New York: Hemisphere, 1989) 192; *Who's Who in the West*, 546.

[43] Sister Mary Anthony Scally, *Negro Catholic Writers: 1940–1943 A Bio-Bibliography* (Detroit: Walter Romig, 1945) 91; Fleming and Burckel, *Who's Who in Colored America*, 1950, 419.

[44] *Macon Telegraph and News*, 21 January 1987.

ten outstanding black women for her outstanding work in civil rights and community development in the Dayton community.[45]

Walter C. Daniel, 1937, held several important positions during a long career in academia. He began his English studies at Johnson C. Smith University (B.A.), continuing at Case Western Reserve, North Dakota State University, and Bowling Green (Ph.D.). Daniel did postdoctoral work in educational management at the Harvard University School of Business. Among the positions he held were vice-chancellor of University of Missouri at Columbia, president of Lincoln University of Missouri in Jefferson City, and chairman of the division of humanities at Saint Augustine's College in Raleigh, North Carolina. Daniel's extensive list of publications includes *Black Journals of the United States* (1982) and *"De Lawd," Richard B. Harrison and The Green Pastures* (1986).[46]

Another Ballardite with a distinguished military record was Colonel Daniel M. Walker, 1937. In addition to receiving a B.A. in social sciences from Talladega College (1942), Walker also attended Shrivenham American University (Oxford, England), Armed Forces Staff College, Army Command and General Staff College, Logistics Management Institute, and the University of Virginia. A thirty-year veteran of the U.S. armed services, Colonel Walker's military assignments included England, France, Belgium, Holland, and Germany. Among his numerous citations were the Legion of Merit with Oak Leaf Cluster, the Bronze Star, and European, African, Middle Eastern, and Vietnam service and campaign medals.[47]

Eldred Davis, 1939, studied English at Georgia State College (now Savannah State) (B.S., 1948) and at the University of Michigan (M.A., 1954; and M.A.L.S. in English education, 1960). After studies in curriculum and instruction at the University of Tennessee (Ed.D., 1968) and additional studies at the University of

---

[45] Mattie Jewel May Davis to Raymond J. Pitts, 10 February 1980, AMAA.
[46] Walter C. Daniel to Raymond J. Pitts, 1979, AMAA.
[47] Daniel M. Walker to Raymond J. Pitts, n.d., AMAA.

Massachusetts, Grambling State University, and the University of Missouri at Rolla, she taught at Ballard-Hudson High School for six years. She held several positions, including dean of the college, and served on the board of trustees as a faculty representative at Knoxville College, Knoxville, Tennessee.[48]

Among the many other Ballardites who deserve mention are John Moore, who became a leading Congregational minister in Texas, and Lorena Kemp, Ph.D., a noted long-time faculty member of West Virginia State College, as well as a host of other individuals who made contributions in the medical profession: Charles Hutchings, J. S. Williams, Jr., Henry Nixons, Edinburgh Hubbard, Jr., George Chapman, Marion Thomas, Charles N. Pitts Jr., Joseph Carwin, Richard Carey Jr., Claudius Jones, Walker Thomas, E.M. Calhoun, and Charles T. Lunsford.[49]

It is clear from the accomplishments of these Ballardites and others not mentioned that they received a good education at Ballard and at Lewis High School.

---

[48] Eldred Davis to Raymond J. Pitts, 20 December 1979, AMAA.

[49] "AMA Makes Contribution to World Through Ballard," *Macon Daily Telegraph*, n.d., AMAA.

BIBLIOGRAPHY

Primary Material

Manuscripts

American Missionary Association Archives. Amistad Research Center, New Orleans, Louisiana. (available on microfilm)

Ballard Normal School Historical Collection. Archives and Genealogy Department, Washington Memorial Library, Macon, Georgia.

Bureau of Refugees, Freedmen and Abandoned Lands. Reports of the Georgia Superintendent of Education, 1865–70. RG 105. National Archives, Washington, D.C. (available on microfilm)

——. Records of the Assistant Commissioner for the State of Georgia, 1865–1869. RG 105. National Archives, Washington, D.C. (available on microfilm)

Office of the Comptroller of the Currency. Registers of Signatures of Depositors in Branches of the Freedman's Savings and Trust Company, 1865–1874. RG 101. National Archives, Washington, D.C. (available on microfilm)

United States Bureau of the Census. Manuscript population schedules for the years 1830, 1840, 1850, 1860, and 1870. National Archives, Washington, D.C. (available on microfilm)

Fred L. Brownlee Papers. Amistad Research Center, New Orleans.

John A. Rockwell Papers. Amistad Research Center, New Orleans.

Raymond G. von Tobel Papers, Amistad Research Center, New Orleans.

Raymond G. von Tobel Diaries, Georgia State Archives, Atlanta, Georgia.

Edmund Asa Ware Papers. Robert W. Woodruff Library, Atlanta University, Atlanta, Georgia.

Government Documents and Annual Reports

Alvord, John W. "Letters from the South Relating to the Condition of Freedmen, Addressed to Major General O.O. Howard, Commissioner, Bureau of Refugees, Freedmen and Abandoned Lands." Washington, D.C.: Howard University Press, 1870.

American Missionary Association. "History of the American Missionary Association with Facts and Anecdotes Illustrating Its Work in the South." New York: S. W. Green, 1874.

American Temperance Union. "Band of Hope Melodies; Adapted to Band of Hope, Cadet and Other Temperance Meetings." New York: American Temperance Union, 1860.

Barnard, Henry. "History of Schools for the Colored Population." *Special Report of the U.S. Commissioner of Education*. Washington, D.C.: Government Printing Office, 1871.

Calvin, Martin V. "Recent Progress of Public Education in the South: A Paper Read Before the Georgia Teachers' Association at Savannah, May 5th, 1870." Augusta: Chronicle and Sentinel Steam Printing Establishment, 1870.

Georgia Equal Rights Association. "Proceedings of the Freedmen's Convention Association among the Freedmen." Boston: South Boston Inquirer Press, 1874.

Georgia, State of. Annual Reports of the State Commissioner of the State of Georgia. 1871–1876 and 1942–1945.

Greenleaf, Walter J. *Junior Colleges*, Bulletin No. 3, United States Department of the Interior. Washington, D.C.: Government Printing Office, 1936.

Illinois, State of. *Blue Book of the State of Illinois*. 1944, 1956.

Jones, Thomas Jessie. *Negro Education: A Study of Private and Higher Schools for Colored People in the United States*. Washington, D.C.: U.S. Government Printing Office, 1901.

Macon/Bibb County Board of Education Annual Reports, 1885–1900 and 1942–1945. Archives and Genealogy Department, Washington Memorial Library, Macon, Georgia.

Mayo, A. D. "Common School Education in the South from the Beginning of the Civil War to 1870–1876." In *Report of the United States Commissioner of Education for the Years 1900–1901*. 2 vols. Washington, D.C.: U.S. Government Printing Office, 1901.

———. "Industrial Education in the South," Bureau of Education, Circular of Information No. 5, 1888. Washington, D.C.: Government Printing Office, 1888.

———. "Work of Certain Northern Churches in the Education of the Freedmen, 1861–1900," *Report of the United States Commissioner of Education for 1901–1902*. 2 vols. Washington, D.C.: Government Printing Office, 1902.

National Youth Administration. *Youth, Jobs and Defense*. Washington, D.C.: Government Printing Office, 1941.

Parmalee, Julius H. "Freedmen's Aid Societies, 1861–1871." In *Negro Education: A Study of the Private and Higher Schools for Colored People in the United*

States, U.S. Department of Interior, Bureau of Education *Bulletin,* 1916.
    Nos. 38, 39. 2 vols. Washington, D.C.: Government Printing Office 1917.
Slater Fund. *Proceedings of the Trustees of the John F. Slater Fund for the Education
    of Freedmen.* 1883, 1888.

Newspapers

Macon *American Union,* 1866–1872
Ballard Normal School *Ballardite,* 1929–1946
Augusta *Colored American,* 1865–1866
Augusta *Daily News,* 1934
Augusta *Loyal Georgian,* 1866–1867
Augusta *News Review,* 1976
*Macon News,*1920s
Macon Telegraph, 1850–1869
Macon Telegraph and News (recent)
New York Times, 1901, 1975

Periodicals/Journals

American Missionary, 1865–1934
Christian Recorder
Freedmen's Journal
The Missionary Herald at Home and Abroad, 1934–1949

Pamphlets

American Missionary Association. "Women Work for the Lowly; as Illustrated in
    the Work of the American Missionary of Georgia, Assembled at Augusta,
    January 10th, 1866." Augusta: Loyal Georgian Press, 1866.
————. "Proceedings of the Convention of the Equal Rights and Educational
    Association of Georgia held in Macon, October 29, 1866." Augusta: Loyal
    Georgian Press, 1866.
Atlanta University Publications. *Social and Physical Condition of Negroes in Cities.*
    No. 2. Atlanta: Atlanta University Press, 1897.
Benjamin Brawley. "Early Effort for Industrial Education." *Occasional Papers,*
    No. 22. The Trustees of the John F. Slater Fund, 1923.
Chase, Thomas N., ed. *Mortality Among Negroes in Cities.* Atlanta University
    Publications, No. 1. Atlanta: Atlanta University Press, 1903.
Conaty, Thomas J. "The Temperance Idea in Public Instruction." Boston:
    Massachusetts State Teachers' Association, 1894.
Du Bois, W. E. B., ed. *The Negro Artisan: A Social Study.* Atlanta University
    Publications, No. 7. Atlanta: University of Atlanta Press, 1902.
Georgia, University of. "The Accredited High Schools of Georgia." *Bulletin of the
    University of Georgia* 35 (September 1934): 8–9.

Mayo, Amory D. "Methods of Moral Instruction in Common Schools." The Addresses and Journals of the Proceedings of the National Educational Association...1872. Peoria IL: N. C. Nason, 1873.

Negro Young Peoples' Christian and Educational Congress. *Official Program and Music of the Negro Young Peoples' Christian and Educational Congress.* Washington, D.C.: I. Garland Penn, 1906.

Pierson, H. W. "A Letter to Hon. Charles Summer with Statements of Outrages Upon Freedmen in Georgia...by the Ku Klux Klan." Washington, D.C.: Washington Chronicle, 1870.

Scally, Sister Mary Anthony. *Negro Catholic Writers: 1940–1943 A Bio-Bibliography.* Detroit: Walter Romig, 1945.

Wright, Richard R. "A Brief Historical Sketch of Negro Education in Georgia." Savannah: Robinson Printing House, 1894.

Books

Adams, Myron W. *A History of Atlanta University, 1865–1929.* Atlanta: Atlanta University Press, 1930.

Anderson, James D. *The Education of Blacks in the South, 1860–1935.* Chapel Hill: University of North Carolina Press, 1988.

Bacote, Clarence A. *The Story of Atlanta University: A Century of Service 1865–1965.* Atlanta: Atlanta University, 1969.

Barrons, Isabel C., ed. *First Mohonk Conference of the Negro Question held at Lake Mohonk, Ulster County, New York, June, 5, 6, 1890.* Boston: George H. Ellis, Printer, 1890.

Beard, Augustus Field. *A Crusade of Brotherhood: A History of the American Missionary Association.* Boston: Pilgrim Press, 1909.

Bentley, George R. *A History of the Freedmen's Bureau.* New York: Octagon Books, 1970.

Boris, Joseph J. *Who's Who in Colored America.* New York: Who's Who in Colored American Corporation, 1928–1929.

Brownlee, Fred L. *New Day Ascending.* Boston: Pilgrim Press, 1946.

Bryan, T. Conn. *Confederate Georgia.* Athens: University of Georgia Press, 1953.

Bullock, Henry Allen. *A History of Negro Education in the South.* Cambridge: Harvard University Press, 1967.

Butchart, Ronald E. *Northern Schools, Southern Blacks, and Reconstruction: Freedmen's Education, 1862–1875.* Westport CT: Greenwood Press, 1980.

Caldwell, A. B. *History of the American Negro and His Institutions.* Georgia Edition. Atlanta: A. B. Caldwell, 1912.

Conway, Alan. *The Reconstruction of Georgia.* Minneapolis: University of Minnesota Press, 1966.

Cox, LàWanda and John H. Cox, eds. *Reconstruction, the Negro, and the New South.* Columbia: University of South Carolina Press, 1973.

Currie-McDaniel, Ruth. *Carpetbagger of Conscience: A Biography of John Emory Bryant.* Athens: University of Georgia Press, 1987.

Dittmer, John. *Black Georgia in the Progressive Era, 1900–1920.* Urbana: University of Illinois Press, 1977.

Douglass, H. Paul. *Christian Reconstruction in the South.* Boston: Pilgrim Press, 1909.

Drago, Edmund L. *Initiative, Paternalism, and Race Relations: Charleston's Avery Normal Institute.* Athens: University of Georgia Press, 1990.

Elson, Ruth Miller. *Guardians of Tradition: American Schoolbooks of the Nineteenth Century.* Lincoln: University of Nebraska Press, 1964.

Fisher, John E. *The John F. Slater Fund: A Nineteenth Century Affirmative Action for Negro Education.* New York: University Press of America, Inc., 1986.

Flanders, Ralph Betts. *Plantation Slavery in Georgia.* Chapel Hill: University of North Carolina Press, 1933.

Fleming, G. James, and Christian E. Burckel. *Who's Who in Colored America.* 7th. ed. New York: Christian E. Burckel and Associates, 1950.

Fleming, Walter L. *The Freedmen's Savings Bank: A Chapter in the Economic History of the Negro Race.* Chapel Hill: University of North Carolina Press, 1927.

Foner, Eric. *Reconstruction. America's Unfinished Revolution: 1863–1877.* New York: Harper and Row, 1988.

Foster, Vera Chandler and W. Hardin Hughes. *Negro Year Book 1941–46.* Alabama: Tuskegee, 1946.

Fraser, Walter J., R. Frank Saunders, Jr., and Jon L. Wakelyn, eds. *The Web of Southern Social Relations. Women, Family, and Education.* Athens: University of Georgia Press, 1985.

Gordon, Asa H. *The Georgia Negro, A History.* Ann Arbor: Edwards Brothers, Inc., 1937.

Grant, Donald L. *The Way It Was in the South: The Black Experience in Georgia.* Edited by Jonathan Grant. Secaucus NJ: Carrol Publishing Group, 1993.

Greene, Harry Washington. *Holders of Doctorates Among American Negroes.* Boston: Meador Publishing Co., 1946.

Hamilton, Green P. *Beacon Lights of the Race.* Memphis: E. H. Clarke and Brother, 1911.

Harlan, Louis R. *Separate and Unequal.* Chapel Hill: University of North Carolina Press, 1958.

Haygood, Atticus G. *Our Brother in Black: His Freedom and His Future.* Nashville: Southern Methodist Publishing House, 1881.

———. *Pleas for Progress.* Nashville: Publishing House of the M.E. Church, South, 1889.

Hine, Darlene Clark, ed. *Black Women in America: An Historical Encyclopedia.* Vol. 2. Brooklyn: Carlson, 1993.

Johnson, Michael P. *Toward a Patriarchal Republic: The Secession of Georgia.*
    Baton Rouge: Louisiana State University Press, 1977.
Joiner, Oscar H., James C. Bonner, H. S. Shearouse, T. E. Smith, eds. *A History of*
    Public Education in Georgia 1734–1976. Columbia SC: R. L. Bryan
    Company, 1979.
Jones, Jacqueline. *Soldiers of Light and Love: Northern Teachers and Georgia*
    Blacks 1865–1873. Chapel Hill: University of North Carolina Press, 1980.
Kousser, J. Morgan. *The Shaping of Southern Politics: Suffrage Restriction and the*
    Establishment of the One-Party South, 1880–1910. New Haven: Yale
    University Press, 1974.
Levine, Lawrence W. *Black Culture and Black Consciousness.* New York: Oxford
    University Press, 1977.
Litwack, Leon. *Been in the Storm So Long. The Aftermath of Slavery.* New York:
    Alfred A. Knopf, 1979.
Logan, Rayford W. and Michael R. Winston. *Dictionary of American Negro*
    Biography. New York: W. W. Norton, 1982.
Macon Guide and Ocmulgee National Monument. Compiled by the workers of the
    federal writers project of the Works Progress Administration in the State of
    Georgia. Macon: J.W. Burke, 1939.
Magdol, Edward. *A Right to the Land: Essays on the Freedmen's Community.*
    Westport CT: Greenwood Press, 1977.
Marsh, J. B. T. *The Story of the Jubilee Singers Including Their Songs.* London:
    Hodder and Stoughton, 1897.
Mather, Frank L., ed. *Who's Who of the Colored Race (1915).* Vol. 1. 1915.
    Reprint, Detroit: Gale Research, 1976.
McFeely, William S. *Yankee Stepfather: General O. O. Howard and the Freedmen.*
    New Haven: Yale University Press, 1968.
McPherson, James M. *The Negro's Civil War.* New York: Vintage Books, 1965.
Morris, Robert C. *Reading, 'Riting, and Reconstruction: The Education of*
    Freedmen in the South, 1861–1870. Chicago: University of Chicago Press,
    1976.
Nathans, Elizabeth Studley. *Losing the Peace: Georgia Republicans and*
    Reconstruction, 1865–1871. Baton Rouge: Louisiana State University Press,
    1968.
Nieman, Donald G. *To Set the Law in Motion: The Freedmen's Bureau and the*
    Legal Rights of Blacks, 1865–1868. Millwood NY: KTO Press, 1979.
Orr, Dorothy. *A History of Education in Georgia.* Chapel Hill: University of North
    Carolina Press, 1950.
Osthaus, Carl R. *Freedmen, Philanthropy, and Fraud: A History of the Freedmen's*
    Savings Bank. Urbana: University of Illinois Press, 1976.
Oubre, Claude F. *Forty Acres and a Mule.* Baton Rouge: Louisiana University
    Press, 1978.

Pitts, Raymond J. *Reflections on a Cherished Past.* Sacramento: By the author, 1980.

Range, Willard. *The Rise and Progress of Negro Colleges in Georgia 1865–1949.* Athens: University of Georgia Press, 1951.

Ransom, Roger L., and Richard Sutch. *One Kind of Freedom: The Economic Consequences of Emancipation.* Cambridge: Cambridge University Press, 1977.

Reidy, Joseph P. *From Slavery to Agrarian Capitalism in the Cotton South: Central Georgia, 1800–1880.* Chapel Hill: University of North Carolina Press, 1992.

Richardson, Joe M. *Christian Reconstruction: The American Missionary Association and Southern Blacks, 1861–1890.* Athens: University of Georgia Press, 1986.

Roark, James L. *Masters without Slaves: Southern Planters in the Civil War and Reconstruction.* New York: W. W. Norton, 1977.

Rubin, Louis D., Jr., ed. *Teach the Freedman: The Correspondence of Rutherford B. Hayes and the Slater Fund for Negro Education.* Vols. 1, 2. Baton Rouge: Louisiana State University Press, 1959.

Sammons, Vivian Ovelton. *Blacks in Science and Medicine.* New York: Hemisphere, 1989.

Simmons, William J. *Men of Mark: Eminent, Progressive and Rising.* 1887. Reprint, New York: Arno, 1968.

Spivey, Donald. *Schooling for the New Slavery: Black Industrial Education, 1868–1915.* Westport CT: Greenwood Press, 1978.

Stanley, A. Knighton. *The Children Is Crying: Congregationalism Among Black People.* New York: Pilgrim Press, 1979.

Stuart, M. S. *An Economic Detour: A History of Insurance in the Lives of American Negroes.* New York: Wendell Malliet, 1940.

Swint, Henry L. *Dear Ones at Home: Letters from Contraband Camps.* Nashville: Vanderbilt University Press, 1966.

———. *The Northern Teacher in the South 1862–1870.* New York: Octagon Books, Inc., 1941.

Thernstrom, Stephan. *Poverty and Progress: Social Mobility in a Nineteenth-Century City.* Cambridge: Harvard University Press, 1964.

Thompson, Clara Mildred. *Reconstruction in Georgia: Economic, Social, Political 1865–1872.* Savannah: Beehive Press, 1972.

Woodward, C. Vann. *The Strange Career of Jim Crow.* New York: Oxford University Press, 1966.

Vaughn, William Preston. *Schools for All: The Blacks and Public Education in the South, 1865–1877.* Lexington: University of Kentucky Press, 1974.

Webber, Thomas L. *Deep Like the Rivers: Education in the Slave Quarter Community 1831–1865.* New York: W. W. Norton, 1978.

Wilkinson, Frederick D. *Directory of Graduates Howard University 1870–1963.* Washington, D.C.: Howard University Press, 1965.

Wolters, Raymond. *The New Negro on Campus: Black College Rebellions of the 1920s.* Princeton: Princeton University Press, 1975.

Woodson, Carter G. *The Education of the Negro Prior to 1861.* 1915. Reprint, Salem NH: Ayer, 1991.

Young, Ida, Julius Gholson, and Clara Nell Hargrove. *History of Macon, Georgia 1823–1949.* Macon: Lyon, Marshall and Brooks, 1950.

Articles

Cimbala, Paul A. "The Talisman Power: Davis Tillson, the Freedmen's Bureau, and Free Labor in Reconstruction Georgia, 1865–866." *Civil War History* 28 (June 1982): 153–71.

Cox, John and LaWanda Cox. "General O. O. Howard and the Misrepresented Bureau." *Journal of Southern History* 19 (February 1953): 427–56.

DuBois, W. E. B. "The Negro Common School, Georgia." *Crisis.* Vol. 32 (September 1926): 254–55.

Lane, David A. "The Junior College Movement Among Negroes." *The Journal of Negro Education* II (January 1933): 274–275, 283.

McPherson, James M. "White Liberals and Black Power in Negro Education, 1865–1915." *American Historical Review* 75 (June 1970): 1357–79.

Matthews, John M. "Negro Republicans in the Reconstruction of Georgia." *Georgia Historical Quarterly* 60 (1976): 145–64.

Nieman, Donald G. "Andrew Johnson, the Freedmen's Bureau, and the Problem of Equal Rights, 1865–1866." *Journal of Southern History* 44 (1978): 399–420.

Parmelee, Julius H. "Freedmen's Aid Societies, 1861–1871." Pages 268–95 in *Negro Education: A Study of the Private and Higher Schools for Colored People in the United States.* Edited by Thomas Jesse Jones. 1917. Reprint, New York: Arno Press, 1969.

Parmet, Robert D. "Schools for the Freedmen." *Negro History Bulletin* 34 (1971): 128–32.

Rabinowitz, Howard N. "Half a Loaf: The Shift from White to Black Teachers in the Negro Schools of the Urban South, 1865–1890." *Journal of Southern History* 40 (November 1974): 565–94.

Small, Sandra E. "The Yankee Schoolmarm in Freedmen's Schools: An Analysis of Attitudes." *Journal of Southern History* 45 (August 1979): 381–402.

Vaughn, William P. "Partners in Segregation: Barnas Sears and the Peabody Fund." *Civil War History* 9 (1964): 260–75.

West, Earle H. "The Harris Brothers: Black Northern Teachers in the Reconstruction South." *Journal of Negro Education* 48 (Spring 1979): 126–38.

Weisenburger, Francis P. "William Sanders Scarborough: Early Life and Years at
     Wilberforce." *Ohio History* 71 (1962): 209.
Williams, W. T. B. "The South's Changing Attitude Toward Negro Education."
     Southern Workman 54 (September 1925): 398–400.

Dissertations and Theses

DeBoer, Clara Merritt. "The Role of Afro-Americans in the Origins and Work of
     American Missionary Association, 1839–1877." Ph.D. dissertation, Rutgers
     University, 1973.
Drake, Richard B. "The American Missionary Association and the Southern
     Negro, 1861–1888." Ph.D. dissertation, Emory University, 1957.
Eaton, James Nathaniel. "The Life of Erastus Milo Cravath: A Guiding Light in
     an Era of Darkness." Master's thesis, Fisk University, 1959.
Johnson, Clifton H. "The American Missionary Association, 1846–1861: A Study
     of Christian Abolitionism." Ph.D. dissertation, University of North
     Carolina, 1958.
Jones, Maxine Deloris. "A Glorious Work: The American Missionary Association
     and Black North Carolinians, 1863–1880." Ph.D. dissertation, Florida State
     University, 1982.
Presley, Susan F. "A Past to Cherish—A Future to Fulfill, Lewis High-Ballard
     Normal School, 1865–1900." Master's thesis, Georgia Southern University,
     1992.
Smith, S. L. "The Relation of Farm Labor to School Term and Attendance."
     Master's Thesis, George Peabody College for Teachers, 1918.
William, Gilbert Anthony. "The A.M.E. Christian Recorder: A Forum for the
     Social Ideas of Black Americans, 1854–1902." Ph.D. dissertation, University
     of Illinois at Urbana-Champaign, 1979.
Wright, C. T. "The Development of Education for Blacks in Georgia,
     1865–1900." Ph.D. dissertation, Boston University, 1977.

INDEX